Thank you for your purchase of *Understanding Today's Global LNG Business*. If you wish to purchase additional copies of this book, please visit our website at www.enerdynamics.com. Or call us at 866.765.5432. Volume discounts start at as few as twenty-five books.

If you enjoyed this book, you may also be interested in our other energy business books: *Understanding Today's Natural Gas Business* and *Understanding Today's Electricity Business*. As with our LNG book, these present a comprehensive industry overview in simple and easy-to-understand language. Priced at $64.95 and $69.95, they are the perfect primers for those new and not-so-new to the energy industry, and provide valuable reference for years to come.

We also invite you to experience other learning opportunities available from Enerdynamics. These include public and in-house seminars, self-paced online training, as well as our free *Energy Insider* newsletter. Learn more about all these products at www.enerdynamics.com.

Understanding Today's Global LNG Business

By Bob Shively, John Ferrare and Belinda Petty

3101 Kintzley Court, Suite F
Laporte, CO 80535
866.765.5432
www.enerdynamics.com

Enerdynamics Corp.

Enerdynamics is an education firm dedicated to preparing energy industry employees for success in a challenging environment. We offer an array of public and in-house educational opportunities including classroom seminars, online seminars, and books. We can be contacted at 866-765-5432 or info@enerdynamics.com. Please visit our website at www.enerdynamics.com

About the Authors

Bob Shively has over 25 years of experience in the gas and electric industries. As a partner in Enerdynamics, Bob has advised and educated some of the largest energy industry participants on issues ranging from market strategies to industry restructuring. Bob began his career in the energy industry at Pacific Gas and Electric Company (PG&E). At PG&E Bob held various positions including Major Account Executive to some of PG&E's largest end-use customers and Director of Gas Services Marketing where he was responsible for product development and sales for the company's $1.5 billion dollar Canadian pipeline project. Bob has Master of Science degrees in both Mechanical and Civil Engineering from Stanford University and is a frequent energy industry speaker

John Ferrare has worked in the energy industry as a marketing and communications specialist for over 15 years. He began his career with Pacific Gas and Electric Company where he was integral in developing the marketing group for the company's Gas Services Marketing Department. In 1995, John joined Enerdynamics to manage its educational services. In this role, he has helped create a comprehensive program to educate 600 utility employees on the changes brought by recent deregulation as well as the core classes currently offered by Enerdynamics. A graduate of Northwestern University's School of Speech, John has also developed and teaches a public speaking and communications class for a variety of corporate audiences.

Belinda Petty has over 20 years of wide-ranging experience in the energy industry. Her broad upstream experience includes developing gathering systems in Oklahoma and managing gas processing assets in 11 western states. Her midstream experience includes distributing and selling liquids on the Dixie and Cherokee pipelines, managing gas supply for Conoco Inc.'s refineries, negotiating gas transportation on interstate pipelines, and selling gas and gas services for Conoco's 100 MMcf/d and Union Pacific's 500 MMcf/d western states gas portfolios. As Area Manager for UP's Gas Marketing group, Belinda developed and implemented a successful growth strategy for a $200 million revenue portfolio targeting wholesale and industrial customers. Belinda holds a Bachelor of Science degree and an MBA from Texas Tech University.

ISBN 978-0-9741744-2-6

Edition 2.0

Copyright ©2010. All rights reserved. No part of this book may be reproduced or transmitted in any form by any means, electronic, mechanical, photocopying, recording, or otherwise, without the prior written permission of Enerdynamics Corp.

While every precaution has been taken in the development of this book, Enerdynamics Corp. makes no warranty as to the accuracy or appropriateness of this material for any purpose. Enerdynamics Corp. shall have no liability to any person or entity with respect to any loss or damage caused or alleged to be caused directly or indirectly by material presented in this book.

The authors of this book wish to thank Tim Collins for the extraordinary illustrations designed for this book. These wonderful images tell so much more than our words ever could.

Bob thanks his parents for instilling in him a lifelong love of learning, and Carol, Jed and Tarah for giving him many reasons to keep learning. John thanks Jesse, Rudy, Cody, and Athena for their hugs and kisses during long hours of editing this book.

And finally, we wish to thank the thousands of participants in Enerdynamics' seminars and programs, who in the last ten years have taught the authors more than we could ever have imagined.

Cover photo credits:

Cover photos 1 and 2 courtesy of BP.

Cover photo 3 courtesy of Woodside.

Enerdynamics would like to express its sincere thanks to both BP and Woodside for their invaluable help in securing these beautiful photos for our cover.

CONTENTS

SECTION ONE: INTRODUCTION 1
   What are Natural Gas and Liquefied Natural Gas? 1
   Why Do We Need LNG? 2
   How LNG is Made and Delivered to Consumers 3
   Measuring LNG 5
   A Brief History of LNG 7
   The Current LNG Marketplace 9

SECTION TWO: WORLD SUPPLY AND DEMAND 13
   World Natural Gas Demand 13
   World Natural Gas Supply 14
   Matching Supply and Demand 15
      Supply and Demand in Europe 16
      Supply and Demand in North America 17
      Supply and Demand in Asia, the Pacific and the Middle East 18
      Supply and Demand in South and Central America 20
      Supply and Demand in Africa 21
   Summary of World Supply and Demand 22

SECTION THREE: LIQUEFACTION 25
   Liquefaction Technology 25
      Removal of Impurities and Recovery of NGLs 25
      Liquefaction of the Methane 27
      Storage and Pumping the LNG into Tankers 28
      Ship Loading Facilities 29
   Liquefaction Plant Costs 29
      Capital Costs 29
      Variable Costs 30
   Liquefaction Infrastructure 30
      Existing Plants 30
      Proposed and Future Plants 32
   Key Issues 32

CONTENTS

SECTION FOUR: SHIPPING 35
Ship Technology 35
The Hull and Containment System 36
Vapor Capture and Cargo Monitoring 38
Propulsion 39
Loading and Unloading 40
Ship Certification 41
Shipping Costs 41
Capital Costs 41
Variable Costs 42
The LNG Fleet 43
The Existing Fleet 43
Future Fleets 44
Key Issues 46

SECTION FIVE: REGASIFICATION 49
Regasification Technology 49
Berthing and Unloading 49
Storage 50
Vaporization 52
Delivery into the Pipeline Grid 53
Offshore Regasification Technology 54
Onshore Regasification Plant Costs 55
Capital Costs 55
Operating Costs 56
Regasification Infrastructure 56
Existing Terminals 56
Future Terminals 57
Future Storage Development 57
Future Offshore Terminals 58
Key Issues 60

SECTION SIX: SAFETY AND ENVIRONMENTAL CONCERNS 63
Safety Issues 63
Physical Properties of LNG 64
Specific Safety Concerns 64
Pool Fires 65
Vapor Cloud Fires 65
Rapid Phase Transition Explosion 66
Additional Hazards of Leaking or Spilled LNG 66

LNG and Terrorism 67
Risks Relative to Other Industries 68
The Historical Safety Record of LNG 69
Handling Safety and Security Issues 70
Environmental Issues 72
Conclusions 72

SECTION SEVEN: REGULATION AND PERMITTING 75
Regulation 75
Liquefaction Facilities 77
Shipping 78
Regasification Facilities 79
Offshore Facilities 82
Permitting 83

SECTION EIGHT: MARKET DYNAMICS 87
The LNG Value Chain 87
Market Participants 90
Contract Structure 91
Risk Management in the LNG Marketplace 96
Financing LNG Projects 98
The Current State of the LNG Market 100

SECTION NINE: THE FUTURE 105
Technology Issues 105
Geopolitical Issues 107
Market Issues 108
Will LNG Demand Continue to Grow? .109
Will Investment be Available to Construct the Necessary Infrastructure? . .109
How Will the LNG Business Adapt to Short-term Markets? 110
How Will Future Prices be Determined? 110
Who Will Dominate the Future Marketplace? 111
Global Gas 111

APPENDIX A: GLOSSARY 115

APPENDIX B: LNG UNITS 125

APPENDIX C: ACRONYMS 127

APPENDIX D: WORLDWIDE LIQUEFACTION TERMINALS..................131

CONTENTS

APPENDIX E: WORLDWIDE REGASIFICATION TERMINALS 137

APPENDIX F: INDEX 143

What you will learn:

- What LNG is

- Why we use LNG

- An overview of how LNG is made and delivered

- The units used to measure LNG

- A history of LNG

- An overview of today's LNG marketplace

SECTION ONE: INTRODUCTION

Natural gas demand worldwide is exploding. Driven by economic growth and the environmental advantages of this clean burning fuel, world consumption of natural gas increased by 33% between 1998 and 2008[1]. This growth is just the beginning. Between 2008 and 2015, world consumption is expected to increase another 17% and by 2030 it is expected to increase by more than 40% over 2008 levels[2]. To meet this new growth alone, over the next 20 years we will need to add new production capabilities nearly equal to current North American and Middle Eastern production combined.

Transportation of these supplies will also present challenges. Unfortunately for consumers, sources of natural gas are often inconveniently located far from areas of consumption. While North American markets have historically been served by Canadian and U.S. production, future continental supplies may be inadequate to serve these markets. Meanwhile Western European consumers, already dependent on significant imports of Russian natural gas, will become even more dependent as demand grows and Northern European supplies decline. And growing economies such as Brazil, China and India will all require new sources of energy. The solution will be twofold. Where geography allows gas to be transported through pipes we will see significant growth in high volume and long distance pipeline networks. But for much of the world the solution lies in liquefied natural gas (LNG), which can be economically transported via tanker.

What are Natural Gas and Liquefied Natural Gas?

Natural gas is a fuel that occurs naturally in underground formations. Raw natural gas is composed primarily of methane, the simplest hydrocarbon, along with heavier and more complex hydrocarbons such as ethane, propane, butane, and pentane. In addition, natural gas typically contains non-flammable components such as nitrogen, carbon dioxide and water vapor and may contain hydrogen sulfide which must be removed for safety and to ensure clean emissions. Raw natural gas is processed to cre-

---

[1] *BP Statistical Review of World Energy 2009.*

[2] U.S. Energy Information Administration (EIA) *International Energy Outlook 2009.*

SECTION ONE: INTRODUCTION

ate the natural gas we burn in our homes and businesses, which consists of at least 90% methane with smaller amounts of ethane and other liquid hydrocarbons.

Natural gas is one of the cleanest commercial fuels available since it produces mostly carbon dioxide and water vapor, plus a small amount of nitrogen oxide and carbon monoxide when burned. Relative to other fossil fuels, the amount of carbon released when natural gas is burned is low. Natural gas is often referred to as a "bridge fuel," meaning that it is the most environmentally benign energy source widely available until we further develop our renewable energy sources. Natural gas currently accounts for almost 24% of world primary energy consumption and is expected to maintain its importance over the forseeable future.

In its natural state at atmospheric pressure and normal temperatures, natural gas is in gaseous form. It is commonly transported via pipeline as it is too voluminous to be practically transported by truck or ship as a gas. When natural gas is cooled below approximately –260 degrees Fahrenheit (–162 degrees Celsius) it becomes liquid and its volume is reduced by a factor of about 610. The resulting liquid is called liquefied natural gas or LNG. Because its volume has been reduced dramatically, LNG can often be economically transported via ship or truck or stored in above ground tanks.

Why Do We Need LNG?

When consumers are located on the same continent as natural gas supplies it is usually most economic to transport the gas in a high pressure underground pipeline from the supply basin to the natural gas distribution system. But if consumers are located long distances from supply (in most cases more than 1,000 miles or 1,600 kilometers) and are separated from that supply by water, it can be more economic to liquefy natural gas for transport by ship. While not common, LNG is occasionally transported by truck when pipeline systems are not available.

LNG is also commonly used to store natural gas. Because of the reduced volume, liquefied natural gas can often be economically stored in above ground tanks. Although we will not cover this use of LNG in this book, LNG storage is often used on gas distribution systems as a means of providing natural gas on peak usage days, especially in areas where underground storage is not available. To store gas in this fashion, a small gas liquefaction plant is placed on the gas distribution system, and on lower usage days gas supplies from the distribution system are liquefied and stored. Then on peak usage days, when flowing supplies are inadequate to serve all the loads, the LNG is heated

> **WHY USE LNG?**
>
> - Economic transport
> - Storage
> - Monetize stranded gas
> - Gain access to supply

and reinjected into the distribution system to meet the increased demand.

Producers located in regions with excess supply (meaning natural gas supplies far exceed the consumer demand that can be reached economically by pipeline) view LNG as a means of accessing world markets. LNG allows producers to sell their gas supplies or "monetize their assets" by delivering them to regions where demand exceeds local supply or where local supply is expensive to exploit. And for consumers located in these regions without adequate local supply, LNG is seen as an economic source of natural gas supplies.

How LNG is Made and Delivered to Consumers

Natural gas is produced from underground reservoirs, brought to the surface and processed to remove impurities. The gas is then most commonly transported to consumers first via a long-distance high pressure pipeline and then via a lower pressure

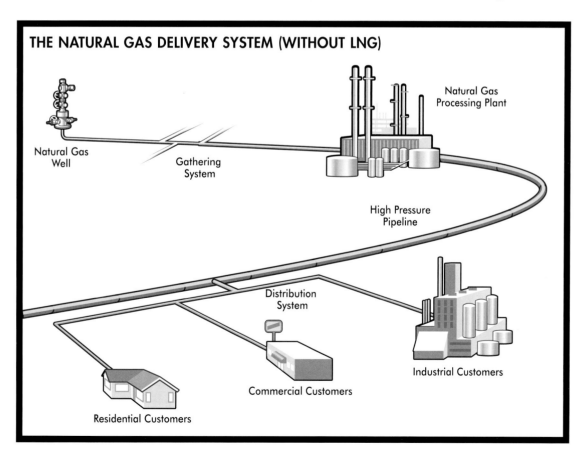

SECTION ONE: INTRODUCTION

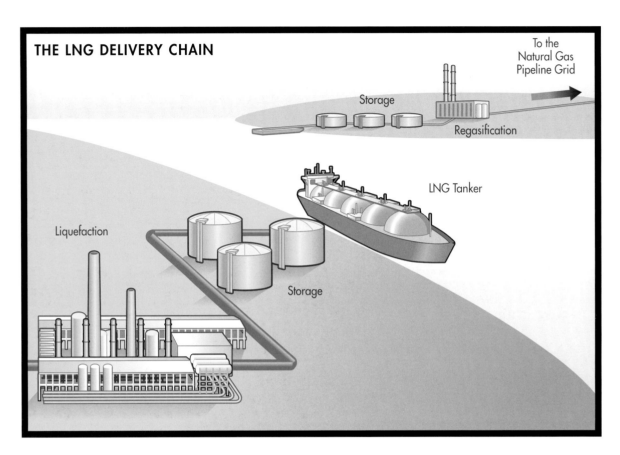

distribution system. In cases where LNG transport is more economic than building a pipeline, the LNG delivery chain is substituted for a portion of the typical pipeline transportation path. Following is a brief discussion of this process. Detailed information on the LNG delivery chain can be found in Sections Three, Four and Five.

To make LNG, natural gas from the production field is first processed and then cooled to –260 degrees Fahrenheit in a liquefaction plant. The LNG is stored at atmospheric pressure in double-walled cryogenic tanks that keep the gas cooled in a liquid state until a tanker is available. LNG is then shipped in an LNG tanker, which is a double-hulled ship specially designed to keep the natural gas cool. Tankers move the LNG from the production area to a regasification terminal near the point of consumption. In most cases, regasification takes place at a terminal although in some cases this process can occur onboard the tanker if it is a regasification vessel. If regasified onboard the vessel, the gas is then put directly into an undersea pipeline that connects to the onshore pipeline grid. In most cases, however, the LNG is off-loaded from the tanker into a storage tank similar to those used at the liquefaction plant. When the gas is needed it is taken from storage and sent through a regasification plant where it is warmed in a carefully controlled environment so that its pressure is increased to match the pressure of the pipeline it will be entering. As the LNG is warmed, it once again assumes its gaseous state. Finally, the gas is put into the pipeline where it is commingled with other gas supplies and delivered to consumers.

Measuring LNG

Before we go on, let's take a moment to discuss the various units used in the LNG industry. This can be complex because different units are used to measure natural gas in its gaseous form and its liquid form, some units are used for both gaseous and liquid form, and since LNG is a global business, we need to consider both English and metric units.

Natural gas is generally measured either by volume or by energy content. When gas is metered, it is usually metered based on volume. Volumetric units typically used are cubic feet (cf), thousands of cubic feet (Mcf), millions of cubic feet (MMcf) and trillions of cubic feet (Tcf) in the English system and cubic meters (m^3), millions of cubic meters, billions of cubic meters, and trillions of cubic meters in the metric system.

NATURAL GAS AND LNG UNIT CONVERSIONS

1 tonne (metric ton) = 2,204.62 lb = 1.1023 short tons

1 kilocalorie (kcal) = 4.187 kilojoule (kJ) = 3.968 Btu

1 Dth = 1 MMBtu = 10 therms = 1,000,000 Btu

1 cubic meter (m^3) = 35.315 Cubic feet (cf)

1 million tonnes (LNG) = 48.7 Bcf* (gas) = 1.379 billion m^3 (gas)

1 Bcf (gas) = 45,000 m^3 (LNG)

1 million tonnes per year (mtpa) (LNG) = 48.7 Bcf/year* (gas) = 1.379 billion m^3/year (gas)

1 tonne (LNG) = 53.57 MMBtu**

* Assumes a specific gravity of LNG at .45
** Assumes a natural gas heating value of 1,100 Btu/cf

Because the energy content (or heating value) of natural gas can vary from one source to the next, a more accurate way of measuring the ultimate value of gas is to use units that measure energy content. For example, you would need less cubic feet of higher heating value gas for a hot shower and, conversely, more of lower heating value gas for the same shower. English units commonly used to measure energy content include British Thermal Units (Btu), millions of Btus (MMBtu), therms, and decatherms (Dth). Metric units used are calories, kilocalories (kcal), joules, kilojoules (kJ), and trillions of joules (TJ).

SECTION ONE: INTRODUCTION

Now that you understand the volumetric and energy content terms used to measure natural gas, we need to add in a few LNG-specific measurements. LNG is generally measured in metric tonnes (which is equal to 2,204.62 pounds) when it is in LNG form, and in cubic feet or cubic meters when converted back to a gaseous state. Annual capacities or flow rates are often stated in terms of million tonnes per annum or million tonnes per year. Various abbreviations are used including mtpa, MMtpa, MMt/y, or million mt/yr. But just to confuse you, tanker capacities are sometimes stated in cubic meters. You have to be careful though, because these are cubic meters of liquid, not gas![3] A typical LNG tanker holds between 120,000 and 145,000 m^3, which is equivalent to 2.7 to 3.2 Bcf (76.5 million to 90.6 million m^3) of gas or 55,400 to 65,700 tonnes of LNG. By way of comparison, one average-sized tanker holds enough natural gas to serve approximately 5% of the United States', 30% of the United Kingdom's or 40% of Japan's average daily consumption. Sizes of new tankers are growing and ships as large as 266,000 m^3 have recently gone into service.

Throughout this book, we will generally use English units of cubic feet and MMBtu to discuss quantities of natural gas consumed or produced. In discussing natural gas as it flows through the LNG value chain, we will use the units most commonly used at that point. For further information, please see Appendix B which contains all the necessary information to make conversions.

Determining the energy content of a volume of LNG is complicated by the fact that the heating value of gas varies depending on where it was produced and how it was processed. A major factor in determining heating value is the amount of natural gas liquids (NGLs) such as ethane, propane and butane that are left in the gas stream. In the United States most of the NGLs are removed from the gas to meet U.S. pipeline specifications. However, the LNG heat content specifications in Asian countries such as Japan and Korea are significantly higher and thus more of the NGLs are left in the gas stream. Additionally, the heating value of an LNG cargo will increase as some of the liquid methane boils off during transport. Typical heating values of LNG cargos range from as high as 1,375 Btu/cf to as low as 1,000 Btu/cf[4]. Thus it is important to establish the heating value of specific cargos before converting from volumetric units to energy-based units. We will discuss this issue further in Section Five.

---

[3] Remember that when liquefied, the volume is reduced by a factor of 610 while the energy content remains the same. So 1 m^3 of LNG holds 610 times the energy content of 1 m^3 of natural gas.

[4] The heating value of typical U.S. pipeline gas is 1,025 Btu/cf.

UNDERSTANDING TODAY'S GLOBAL LNG BUSINESS

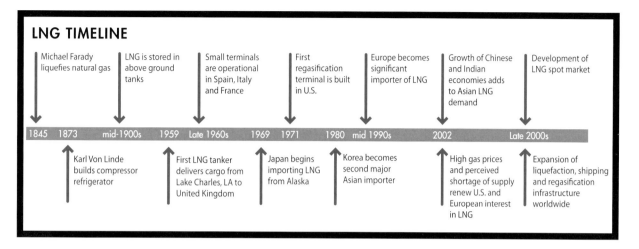

A Brief History of LNG

Natural gas liquefaction was first demonstrated by British scientist Michael Faraday in 1845. The first practical compressor refrigeration machine for natural gas was built in Germany in 1873 by engineer Karl Von Linde and by the mid-1900s LNG plants were in commercial use to allow above-ground storage of natural gas. In 1959 the world's first LNG tanker, a converted World War II Liberty freighter called The Methane Pioneer successfully carried an LNG cargo from Lake Charles, Louisiana to Canvey Island in the United Kingdom. And over the next 14 months, seven additional cargos were delivered. These early voyages proved the viability of LNG transportation and in 1964 the United Kingdom began receiving regular shipments from Algeria.

By the late 1960s and early 1970s small terminals were operational in Spain, Italy and France. However, cheaper pipeline supplies from Northern Europe and later the Soviet Union supplanted much of the LNG trade in the European market,

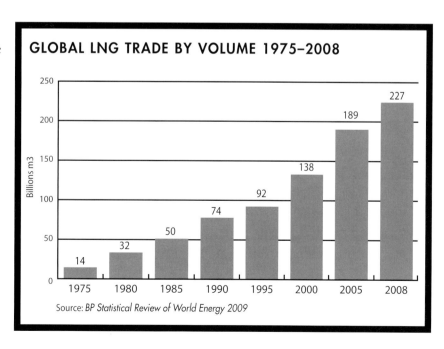

SECTION ONE: INTRODUCTION

leaving continued growth to Asian markets. In 1969 Japan began importing LNG from Alaska. Following the Oil Crisis of 1973 Japan expanded its LNG capabilities, building new terminals and contracting for supplies from various countries including Australia, Brunei, Indonesia, Malaysia, Qatar, and the United Arab Emirates (UAE). Korea become the second major Asian importer in 1980 followed by Taiwan in 1990, leading Asia to dominate world LNG consumption. The U.S. looked poised to join the league of major LNG importers in the 1970s. Four terminals were constructed between 1971 and 1980, but then were quickly mothballed or used minimally as a gas surplus (due to growth in domestic production) developed in North America. By the late 1980s, countries in Europe that were further from the vast Russian gas fields regained interest in LNG. By the mid-1990s Europe – led by Spain, France, Italy, Turkey, and Belgium – became a significant consumer of LNG.

In the early 2000s interest in LNG again grew, driven by rapid demand growth, rising gas prices, and perceptions that some traditional sources of natural gas supply were waning. Trading of LNG volumes grew by 64% between 2000 and 2008. Growth in demand for natural gas led to Argentina, Brazil, China, India, and Mexico joining the ranks of importers, the U.K. rejoining after earlier dismantling its facility, and expansion of LNG import capabilities in many European countries and the U.S. Many existing exporting countries expanded liquefaction capacities and Australia, Equatorial Guinea, Egypt, Norway, and Oman joined the ranks of LNG exporters. During this time period some

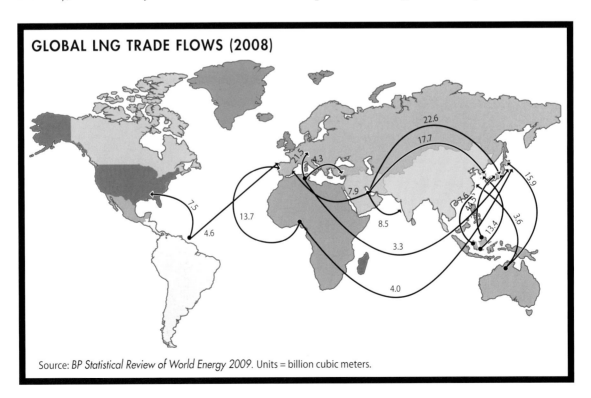

Source: *BP Statistical Review of World Energy 2009*. Units = billion cubic meters.

exporting countries had excess supply leading to a new phenomenon – an LNG spot market. This was a significant change from the traditional practice of long-term contracts between producers and consumers that kept most supply locked up. At times LNG prices fell below the price of pipeline gas in the U.S. and Europe, leading to increased imports in these regions. Later in the decade, LNG supplies became tight relative to demand. LNG prices soared along with oil resulting in LNG consumption only where no alternatives existed. Demand in Asia became a strong factor and many LNG cargos were re-directed to Japan, South Korea and the growing economies of China and India. As of early 2010, a new wave of LNG supply was poised to enter the market, and the supply/demand balance appeared to be swinging back towards a robust supply situation.

The Current LNG Marketplace

By 2008 annual world trade in LNG had grown to an all-time high of 227 billion m^3 (about 8,000 Bcf). Total world liquefaction capacity was approximately 317 billion m^3 per year (11,200 Bcf), about 330 LNG ships were in service, and world regasification capacity was approximately 772 billion m^3 per year (about 27,250 Bcf). As of early 2010, additional construction in liquefaction, shipping and regasification infrastructure was underway. And as the balance between supply and demand fluctuates, and flexibility in contracts and technology grows, the LNG market continues to evolve.

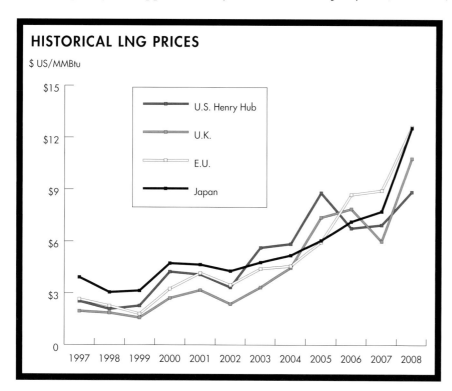

The global LNG market is split into two distinct geographical markets: the Atlantic Basin and the Pacific Basin. The Atlantic Basin includes consumers in Europe and eastern North and South America. This market is supplied by countries in North Africa, West Africa, the Middle East, as well as by Norway and Trinidad. The Pacific Basin has historically been supplied by Indonesia, Malaysia, Australia, Brunei, the U.S.

SECTION ONE: INTRODUCTION

(Alaska), and the Middle East. But in recent years Atlantic Basin supplies from various African countries have begun to flow to Pacific Basin consumers. In 2008, 70% of the world LNG market flowed to the Pacific Basin.

Sellers of LNG and owers of liquefaction facilities are dominated by national oil companies (NOCs) and large gas producers. Owners of ships can be either buyers or sellers, or in many cases independents selling charter services. Buyers of LNG and owners of regasification facilities range from national energy companies to utilities and gas marketing companies. In much of Asia, utilities or national energy companies are the dominant buyers. Meanwhile in Europe and North America, buyers are becoming increasingly dominated by gas marketing companies, largely due to the deregulation of domestic gas markets.

Contracts between buyers and sellers are typically long-term take-or-pay arrangements with a specified delivery market. However, evolution in markets has resulted in some contracts allowing for cargos to be redirected to more profitable markets at times. In some cases this includes excess LNG production not committed to long-term deals. The result has been the evolution of an LNG spot market. However, approximately 80% of LNG supplies remain committed in long-term arrangements.

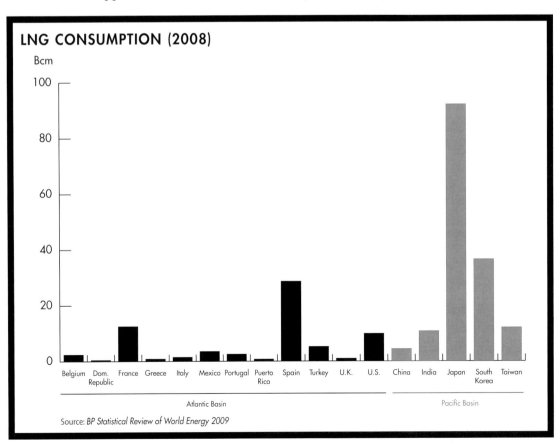

UNDERSTANDING TODAY'S GLOBAL LNG BUSINESS

LNG prices are typically set in one of two ways. For much of Asia as well as most of Europe – except for the U.K. and Belgium – LNG is priced using a formula that is indexed to oil prices. For the U.K, Belgium and the U.S., LNG is usually priced based on market prices in the consuming country. Either way, prices fluctuate significantly depending on market conditions.

As of early 2010, continued growth is expected. New liquefaction facilities are under construction in Algeria, Angola, Australia, Iran, Norway, Peru, and Qatar. If all this planned construction is completed, the result will be an additional annual capacity of 95.3 billion m^3 (3,355 Bcf) by 2012. 38 new LNG ships were delivered in 2009 with over 40 additional ships on order. New or expanded regasification terminals are under construction in Chile, China, India, Italy, Japan, Mexico, the Netherlands, Spain, Thailand, the United Kingdom, and the United States, which will add an additional annual capacity of 115 billion m^3 (4,060 Bcf). Indeed, most observers believe that we are well on our way to a new global gas marketplace – one that may soon rival the complexities and rewards of the petroleum industry.

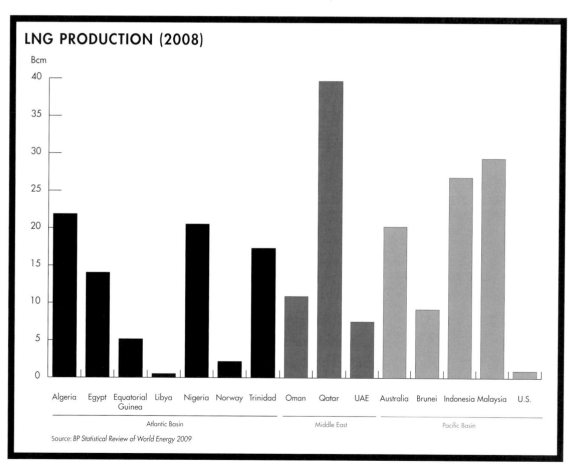

What you will learn:

- Gas consumption levels in various regions of the world
- Where gas reserves and production are located
- How supply and demand are matched in various markets
- The future outlook for supply and demand
- Why LNG is critical to matching global supplies to the largest natural gas consuming countries

SECTION TWO: WORLD SUPPLY AND DEMAND

World Natural Gas Demand

Natural gas is a critical component of the world energy mix. In 2008, the world used approximately 106 Tcf of natural gas, which accounts for nearly 24% of the world's total primary energy supply. This places natural gas third in energy sources behind oil (35%) and coal (28%)[1]. Natural gas use has grown significantly over recent decades, more than tripling since 1970. Most forecasts indicate that natural gas will be one of the fastest growing primary energy sources over the next 20 years, with demand increasing by more than 30%[2]. Much of this growth will come from developing nations, especially China and India. But the industrialized nations are also expected to increase their use of natural gas as environmental concerns result in switching from coal and oil use for industrial production and electric generation.

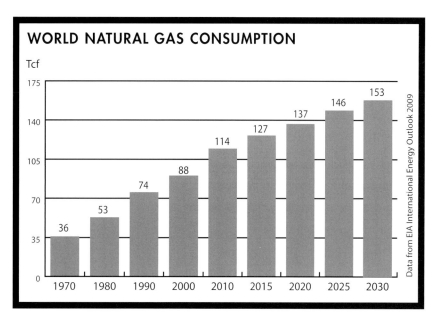

Currently, over 65% of the world's natural gas is consumed in either North America or in Europe, with lesser but significant consumption occurring in Asia and the Middle East. Natural gas is used by residential, commercial, industrial, and power plant consumers. Residential consumers use natural gas mostly for heating

---

[1] BP *Statistical Review of World Energy 2009*.

[2] Energy Information Administration (EIA) *International Energy Outlook 2009*.

SECTION TWO: WORLD SUPPLY AND DEMAND

(both water and space heating) as well as for cooking. Much of commercial use is similar to residential use, with the addition of small production processes. In many countries industrial demand is the most dominant use of natural gas. Approximately 36% of world natural gas demand is for industrial uses such as process heat, boilers, cogeneration, and feedstock[3]. Natural gas is also an important fuel for electricity generation, and this is expected to grow significantly throughout most regions of the world. It is important to remember that natural gas consumption varies significantly at various times during the year and at various locations. Because of significant usage for space heating, world gas demand peaks during the Northern Hemisphere's winter requiring use of storage or flexible production to ensure that gas supplies match demands. There is also a secondary peak during the summer which is due to high use of gas-powered electric generation.

TOP TEN NATURAL GAS CONSUMING COUNTRIES[5]

		Tcf/yr
1.	United States	23.1
2.	Russia	14.8
3.	Iran	4.1
4.	Canada	3.5
5.	United Kingdom	3.3
6.	Japan	3.3
7.	Germany	2.9
8.	China	2.8
9.	Italy	2.7
10.	Saudi Arabia	2.7

World Natural Gas Supply

Since the mid-1970s, world natural gas reserves have steadily grown. As of 2008, world reserves were estimated to be over 6,500 Tcf (the equivalent to over 60 years' worth of world consumption)[4]. This is a significant increase over the 1975 reserve estimate of 2,545 Tcf. Most of this increase has come from development of reserves in the Middle East, Africa and the former Soviet Union. Many forecasts indicate that significant unproved and undiscovered resources also exist. The majority of this gas is expected to be found in the same regions where we have seen recent reserve increases. 53% of the world's gas reserves reside in three countries – Russia, Iran and Qatar – with significant reserves also located elsewhere in the Middle East and in Northern Africa. With

TOP TEN COUNTRIES WITH NATURAL GAS RESERVES

		Tcf
1.	Russia	1,529
2.	Iran	1,046
3.	Qatar	899
4.	Turkmenistan	281
5.	Saudi Arabia	267
6.	United States	238
7.	United Arab Emirates	227
8.	Nigeria	184
9.	Venezuela	171
10.	Algeria	159

---

[3] IEA *Key World Statistics 2009*.

[4] *BP Statistical Review of World Energy 2009*.

[5] All Top Ten data on pages 14 and 15 is for year 2008 from *BP Statistical Review of World Energy 2009*.

the exception of Western Europe and the United States, most areas of the world have yet to produce more than a small percentage of the total amount of natural gas estimated to exist within their borders. The Energy Information Administration (EIA) estimates that the U.S. has already produced more than 40% of its total natural gas resources, leading many to

> **NATURAL GAS RESERVES, RESOURCES AND PRODUCTION**
>
> **Reserves** — Estimated quantities of natural gas that are recoverable from known reservoirs under existing accessibility, economic and technical conditions.
>
> **Resources** — Estimated quantities of natural gas, discovered or undiscovered, that can reasonably be expected to exist in subsurface accumulations. Resources may or may not have been proven to exist by drilling.
>
> **Production** — The amount of natural gas that is taken out of a reserve and made available to the marketplace within a defined period of time.

believe that natural gas is becoming scarce. In fact, when viewed from a global perspective, the opposite is true. Natural gas supply is plentiful, though reserves may not be conveniently located near where consumers live and work.

Matching Supply and Demand

There are three physical components to the delivery system that are key to matching supply and demand. The first is the necessary infrastructure to provide for production (wells, gathering pipelines and processing facilities). The second is the necessary transportation infrastructure to move supply to consumers. And the third is access to storage that allows supply to be adjusted to match seasonal and daily variations in demand. Transportation is typically provided solely through pipelines and distribution lines if supply and demand regions are in relative proximity. But if supply and demand are separated by greater distances this critical component can be provided by tankers carrying LNG.

TOP TEN NATURAL GAS PRODUCING COUNTRIES

		Tcf/yr
1.	Russia	21.2
2.	United States	20.5
3.	Canada	6.2
4.	Iran	4.1
5.	Norway	3.5
6.	Algeria	3.0
7.	Saudi Arabia	2.7
8.	Qatar	2.7
9.	China	2.7
10.	Indonesia	2.4

The key to evaluating the supply/demand situation within a specific country or region is to consider consumption rates relative to production rates, and production rates relative to existing reserves and new reserves additions. Countries with high consumption relative to production must depend on natural gas imports to satisfy customer demand, while countries with high production relative to demand are dependent on export sales for a key source of national income. Countries with falling reserves/production ratios (meaning that new reserves additions are not keeping up with current production) are faced with increasing natural gas imports in the future (if they are a consuming country) or falling export income (if they are a producing country). LNG is important as a source of import gas for consuming countries without adequate domestic or imported pipeline supplies and is also important for countries with excess supply as a source of income. As you can see, the supply/demand situation for a specific country or region of the world quickly tells us how important LNG will be to that area. Following are assessments for specific world regions.

Supply and Demand in Europe

Gas reserves in Europe make up 34% of world reserves, while consumption is almost 38% and production is 35% of world levels[6]. Demand in Europe is driven by the industrialized economies of Western Europe as well as Eastern European countries that often make use of domestic supplies or supplies from neighboring countries. The largest consumer is Russia, though its consumption has decreased since the fall of the Soviet Union. Other large consumers include Belarus, Belgium, France, Germany, Italy, Kazakhstan, the Netherlands, Spain, Turkey, Turkmenistan, the Ukraine, the U.K., and Uzbekistan. Demand by Western European countries is expected to increase – especially in Germany, the U.K. and Spain as these countries adjust their electric generation mixes due to concerns over greenhouse gases and as deregulated gas markets provide opportunities for increased use of natural gas by industrial customers. Overall, it is expected that consumption of natural gas in Europe will grow by approximately 1% per year over the 25 years from 2006 to 2030.

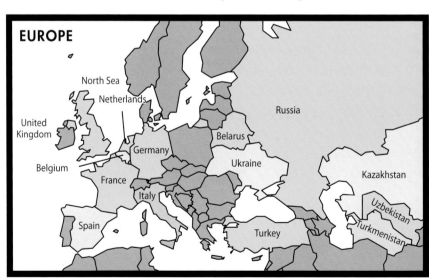

---

[6] All future projection statistics are taken from the EIA's *International Energy Outlook 2009*. And all reserves, consumption and production numbers are from the *BP Statistical Review of World Energy 2009*.

Supply within Europe is dominated by three main sources – North Sea supply controlled by Norway, the Netherlands and the U.K., vast reserves in Russia, and developing reserves in Eurasian countries such as Kazakhstan, Turkmenistan, and Uzbekistan. Production in the North Sea is expected to decline in future years, while production from Russia and the Eurasian countries is expected to grow rapidly. Currently, Western Europe imports over 40% of its supplies. Pipelines from Russia, Algeria and Libya provide over half of the imports while most of the rest comes from LNG imports from Algeria, Equatorial Guinea, Egypt, Libya, Nigeria, Oman, Qatar, and Trinidad and Tobago. But by 2025 the amount imported is forecast to be as high as 59%. Meanwhile, Russia is aggressively moving forward with development of its vast resources and is attempting to negotiate agreements that could result in Russian supply moving by pipeline and/or LNG to virtually all major importing regions of the world. Over the 25 years from 2006 to 2030, gas production in Western Europe is expected to decline slightly while production in the former Soviet Union countries increases by 1.2% per year.

Existing LNG import facilities now operate in Belgium, France, Greece, Italy, Portugal, Spain, Turkey, and the U.K. In the future it is expected that an additional pipeline from Russia will be built into Germany, and other pipelines may be built from Eurasia or North Africa. LNG import facilities are under construction in Italy, the Netherlands, Spain, and the U.K. Meanwhile, both Norway and Russia have recently opened LNG export facilities. Norway is targeting markets in Spain, France and the U.S. while Russia is targeting markets in Asia and the U.S.

Supply and Demand in North America

Gas reserves in North America make up just 5% of world reserves, while consumption and production are a whopping 28% and 27% of world levels. Demand in North America is driven largely by the United States which is the largest natural gas consumer in the world and is responsible for 24% of world consumption. Canada, the fourth largest world consumer, is responsible for just 3% of world consumption, while Mexican consumption represents less

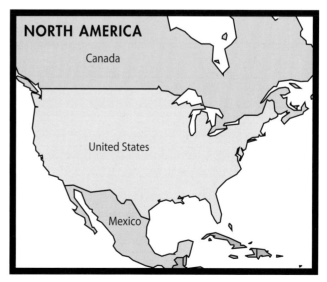

than 2% of world demand. Demand in the U.S. is expected to increase by about 0.5% per year over the 25 years from 2006 to 2030. Canadian consumption is expected to grow by 1.5% annually over the same time period while Mexico's consumption grows more rapidly at a rate of 2.7% per year. Much of Mexican and U.S. demand growth will be driven by gas-fired power plants, while Canadian demand will be increased by use of natural gas for oil production in the Alberta oil sands region. Overall gas consumption in North America is expected to grow by 0.8% per year.

Canada, Mexico and the U.S. all have significant amounts of natural gas supply. The U.S. is the world's second largest gas producer while Canada is the third. Mexico has significant natural gas reserves but has only just begun to develop its production capability and pipeline infrastructure. In future years it is expected that Canadian imports to the U.S. will decline, but U.S. production has recently increased with the development of unconventional reserves such as shale gas. Over the period from 2006 to 2030 it is expected that North American production will grow by about the same level as demand, 0.8% per year.

Historically, North American production has been sufficient to meet demand. Canada serves all its demand through domestic production and in recent years has provided about 15% to the U.S. supply mix. Up until the last few years, the U.S. provided the remainder of its supply domestically. But beginning in 2001 the U.S. restarted imports of LNG, and in recent years 1 to 3% of U.S. supply was being imported as LNG. Mexico has significant natural gas reserves but has not developed the infrastructure to serve all domestic demand. Thus Mexico has imported gas from the U.S. along border areas and began importing LNG in 2006. A number of new LNG terminals have been recently built or are under construction. As of early 2010, operational import terminals in North America included ten in the U.S., two in Mexico, and one each in Canada and the Dominican Republic. Additional terminals under construction included one in Mexico as well as three in the U.S.

Supply and Demand in Asia, the Pacific and the Middle East

Gas reserves in Asia, the Pacific and the Middle East make up 49% of world reserves, while consumption and production are just 27% and 26% of world levels. Demand is highest in the Middle Eastern countries as most major oil producing countries have stressed consumption of natural gas to free up more oil for export. Key demand centers include Iran, Saudi Arabia and the UAE in the Middle East and Australia, China, India, Indonesia, Japan, Malaysia, Pakistan, South Korea, Taiwan, and Thailand in Asia and the Pacific. Consumption in the region is expected to grow significantly.

UNDERSTANDING TODAY'S GLOBAL LNG BUSINESS

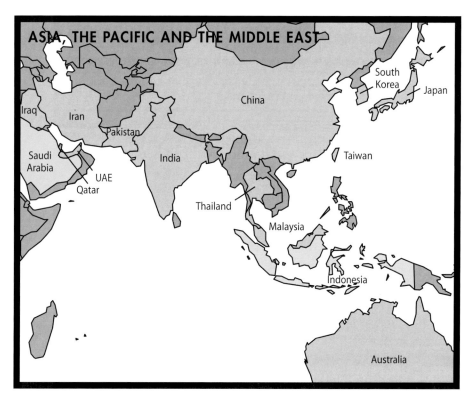

While the more mature economies of Australia, Japan and South Korea are expected to see annual increases of 1% over the 25 years from 2006 to 2030, the developing economies in Asia and the Pacific are expected to see annual demand increases of over 4%. This is about twice as rapid as natural gas demand increases elsewhere in the world. Much of this growth will come from China and India which are expected to see annual demand growth rates of 5.2% and 4.2% respectively. Much of the growth in Asia will feed increasing industrial needs and power generation, but improvements in living standards will also contribute to increased residential usage in urban areas. Growth rates in Middle Eastern countries are expected to be lower, but still significant, at 2% per year.

Almost half of the world's natural gas reserves exist within this region, with over 40% in the Middle East alone. Countries with large amounts of proven reserves include Iran, Iraq, Qatar, Saudi Arabia, the UAE, Australia, Indonesia, and Malaysia. With the exception of Iraq, each of these countries currently exports excess supplies. Production from these countries (again perhaps with the exception of Iraq) is expected to grow significantly in future years as new LNG facilities are constructed and Iran moves forward with a number of proposed pipeline projects. China and India have until recently supplied their demand with internal gas resources, but have now begun to utilize LNG imports. Although these countries are expected to increase production as this demand increases, the size of their reserves base is small relative to growing demand. Overall, production is expected to grow by about 3% per year in Asia, 4% per year in the Pacific and about 2.7% per year in the Middle East over the period 2006 to 2030.

19

SECTION TWO: WORLD SUPPLY AND DEMAND

Demand in the Middle East, Australia, Indonesia, and Malaysia is met with domestic supplies delivered by pipeline. Demands in India, China and Thailand are outstripping domestic supply and imports by pipeline and LNG are now required. Japan, South Korea and Taiwan serve most of their demand with LNG imports and are by far the world's largest market for LNG. China, India, Japan, South Korea, and Taiwan import LNG from a variety of sources including the Middle Eastern countries of Oman, Qatar and the UAE, the African countries of Algeria, Egypt, Equatorial Guinea, and Nigeria, as well as the North American countries of Trinidad and Tobago and the U.S.

The future of this region will be marked by rapid expansion of gas production capability in the Middle Eastern countries and Australia coupled with intense competition between China, India, Japan, and South Korea for access to supply. The producing countries are expected to rapidly expand LNG export capabilities and to send supplies to the U.S. and Mexico, while also expanding sales to Asia. A number of LNG liquefaction projects in both Middle Eastern and Pacific countries are either planned or underway as are regasification projects in China, India, Japan, and Thailand. Iran is expected to focus on the development of both pipelines and LNG. Iran currently sells natural gas to Turkey via pipeline and is developing plans for a major pipeline through Pakistan into India. In addition to depending on LNG supplies from within the region, China, Japan and South Korea are also competing to attract new Russian supplies through pipelines and/or LNG.

Supply and Demand in South and Central America

Gas reserves in South and Central America make up just 4% of world reserves, and consumption and production are both approximately 5% of world levels. Key consuming countries include Argentina, Brazil, Chile, Colombia, and Venezuela. Producing countries include Argentina, Bolivia, Brazil, Colombia, Peru, Trinidad and Tobago, and Venezuela. Much of this production serves domestic needs, although gas is moved by pipeline from Argentina and Bolivia to Brazil, Chile and Uruguay. Trinidad and Tobago also exports LNG to multiple markets. Demand in this region is expected to

increase by 2.4% per year over the 25 years from 2006 to 2030 and production is expected to be sufficient to meet demands. Some countries may utilize LNG imports as an alternative to building pipelines through rugged terrain. As of 2010, Argentina, Brazil and Chile had LNG import terminals in operation and an export terminal was under construction in Peru. The potential for future development of reserves for export purposes appears promising. Future LNG exports may come from Bolivia, Venezuela and Peru. Production in South and Central America is expected to increase by 2.5% per year over the 25 years from 2006 to 2030.

Supply and Demand in Africa

Gas reserves in Africa make up almost 8% of world reserves, while consumption makes up about 3% and production is approximately 7% of world levels. The two largest consumers are Algeria and Egypt which together account for almost 70% of African demand. Demand is expected to grow by 3% per year over the 25 years from 2006 to 2030. In recent years, Africa has continued to grow as an important exporter of natural gas. Algeria, Egypt, Equatorial Guinea, Libya, and Nigeria all export LNG to diverse markets in Asia, Europe and North America. In addition, Algeria exports gas by pipeline to Italy, Portugal and Spain. Egypt exports by pipeline to Jordan, and Libya exports by pipeline to Italy. There are currently five LNG export terminals in Algeria, two in Egypt, four in Nigeria, and one each in Equatorial Guinea and Libya.

A new terminal is under construction in Angola and a terminal in Algeria is under reconstruction to further expand the country's export capacity. Additional export pipelines are under construction or in planning including a new pipeline from Algeria to Spain and Italy, an Egypt to Turkey pipeline with extensions into Eastern Europe, a Libya to Greece pipeline, and a pipeline from Nigeria to Algeria that would allow Nigerian gas to flow to Europe via the Algerian pipeline network. Production in Africa is expected to increase by 3.2% per year over the period 2006 to 2030.

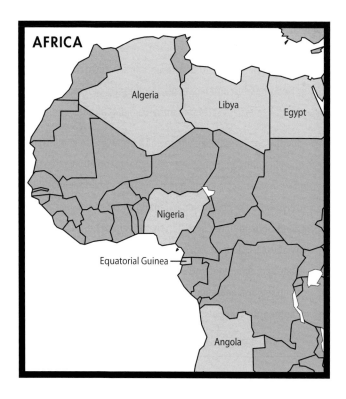

SECTION TWO: WORLD SUPPLY AND DEMAND

Summary of World Supply and Demand

Demand for natural gas is expected to grow worldwide as developing countries join the world economy and as the industrialized countries move away from consumption of coal for electric generation. Future supplies will increasingly come from regions that are remote from the major demand centers. The traditional major demand centers of North America, Western Europe and Northeast Asia will be joined by India and China in requiring more and more imported supplies of natural gas. The likely result is a global natural gas market dominated by long-distance pipelines and an LNG business that begins to resemble today's dynamic and volatile oil marketplace.

OVERVIEW OF WORLD SUPPLY/DEMAND SITUATION

	Reserves	Annual Consumption	Annual Production
Europe	2,221	40	38
North America	313	29	29
Asia, the Pacific and the Middle East	3,224	29	28
South and Central America	258	5	6
Africa	518	3	8

All quantities in Tcf. 2008 data from *BP Statistical Review of World Energy 2009*

What you will learn:

- How natural gas is cooled and liquefied
- The three basic steps in the liquefaction process
- Typical costs of liquefaction
- Where liquefaction plants exist today and where new plants have been proposed
- The key issues affecting future liquefaction development

SECTION THREE: LIQUEFACTION

As you learned in the last Section, the LNG delivery chain (liquefaction, shipping and regasification) replaces the transportation function generally attributed to interstate pipelines. In the first step, liquefaction, natural gas is converted from its gaseous state to a liquid state so that it can be transported via tanker. In the simplest of terms, the liquefaction process takes raw feed gas, removes impurities and other components, cools the gas until it liquefies, and finally moves the liquid into storage tanks. The LNG is then loaded onto tankers for transportation to market. While this sounds reasonably simple, the actual process is quite a bit more complex. In this Section we will explore the technology and costs associated with the liquefaction process. We will also discuss both existing and planned liquefaction infrastructure around the world as well as the key issues affecting the future of liquefaction.

Liquefaction Technology

The three basic steps of the liquefaction process are as follows:

1. Removal of impurities and recovery of natural gas liquids (NGLs)
2. Refrigeration of the gas until it liquefies
3. Movement of the LNG to storage and ultimately into the tanker

Removal of Impurities and Recovery of NGLs

The gas supply that comes from the production field is called raw feed gas. This is typically made up of methane; other hydrocarbons such as ethane, propane, butane, and/or pentane; and substances such as water, sulfur, mercury, and other impurities. The raw feed gas is delivered via pipeline to a processing plant. Here the gas is processed to remove impurities as well as valuable NGLs. The first step is pretreatment, which includes the removal of acid gas such as carbon dioxide and sulfur, as well as mercury and other substances. All of these must be removed either because their freezing points are well above the temperature of the final LNG product (and they could freeze and damage equipment during the cooling process), or because they are impurities that must be removed to meet pipeline specifications at the delivery point. Next water is removed.

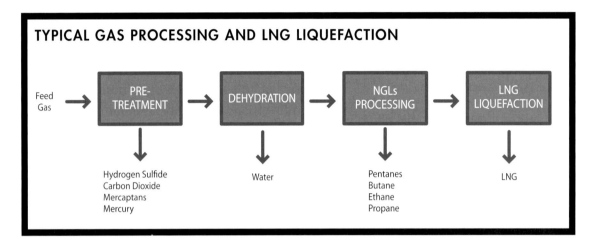

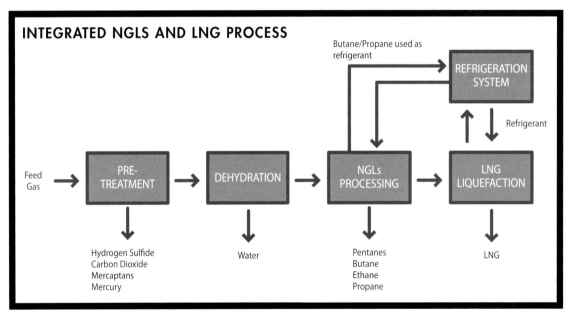

After the above steps, the NGLs such as ethane, propane, butane, and pentanes (also known as heavy hydrocarbons) are removed and collected. In many cases the gas is processed upstream of the liquefaction unit, using traditional gas processing technology (i.e., the same processing that is done to any gas entering an interstate pipeline system). In other cases, the NGLs recovery may be done as an integral step in the liquefaction process. The NGLs collected are valuable products in their own right, and may also be used as refrigerants for the liquefaction process or may be reinjected into the

LNG stream at a later point to adjust the Btu content and flammability characteristics of the LNG. Pentanes and other heavy hydrocarbons are generally exported as a gasoline product. Butane and propane are often also exported as separate products and/or used as refrigerants. Ethane is often reinjected into the LNG stream and may also be used as a refrigerant.

Liquefaction of the Methane

Next, the methane along with any reinjected components, is further cooled to –260 degrees Fahrenheit using LNG liquefaction technology. In this step, the methane mixture liquefies into the final cryogenic liquid state. Although slightly different processes are used in various liquefaction facilities, the basic cooling and liquefaction principles of each process are the same. The key technology is multiple heat exchangers. Here, a cold liquid refrigerant is passed through cooling coils and the natural gas stream is allowed to flow over them, resulting in cooling of the gas stream. As the temperature drops to about –260 degrees Fahrenheit, the gas becomes liquid and can then be pumped into a storage tank.

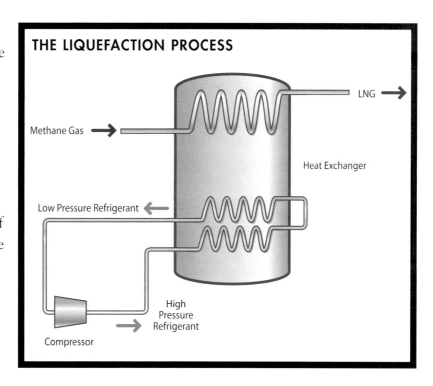

An additional key technology is the drive train for the compressor that pressurizes the refrigerant. Most earlier liquefaction plants were built using steam turbines. But beginning in the late 1980s, gas turbine drive became the norm and most facilities constructed since then have utilized gas turbines. The recently constructed Snohovit plant in Norway used a third alternative – electric drive – so as to minimize greenhouse gas emissions. Compressor sizing and layout is a facility-specific design decision.

SECTION THREE: LIQUEFACTION

Different liquefaction processes include the APCI MCR (Air Products and Chemicals, Inc. Multi-Component Refrigerant) Process, the Phillips Optimized Cascade Process, and various mixed refrigerant processes. The processes differ by type of refrigerant used and by design of the cooling stages. Since each process is proprietary and owned by a specific company, the choice of what process to use is critical since it will tie the plant owner to a specific technology licensee for the life of the plant. Over 80% of the liquefaction plants use the APCI MCR technology. This process uses pre-cooling with propane followed by final cooling with the proprietary refrigerant. A variation called the APCI AP-X process, currently under construction in Qatar, will allow train sizes to increase to 8 mpta. The Phillips Optimized Cascade Process is in use in four existing plants. This process uses three refrigerants to progressively cool the gas. Mixed refrigerant processes use different refrigerants mixed together in various stages. Current mixed refrigerant processes in use or under construction include the Shell dual mixed-refrigerant (DMR) process and the Statoil-Linde mixed-fluid (MCF) process.

The process ultimately chosen is a design decision and depends on various factors including the composition of the feed gas, the availability of refrigerants, whether the NGLs are being removed upstream, the size of the facility, requirements for operational flexibility, and the cost/availability of power for compressors.

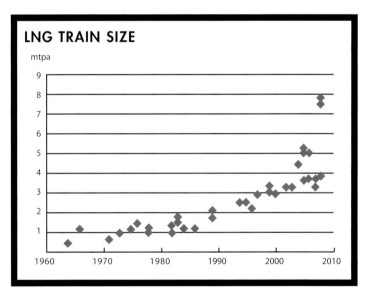

Liquefaction facilities are generally constructed in modular units called trains. A train is a complete standalone processing unit, but often multiple trains are built side-by-side. Train sizes currently range from less than 1 to 8 mtpa. The larger train sizes are becoming common in new plants as engineers attempt to take advantage of economies of scale.

Storage and Pumping the LNG into Tankers

After the liquefaction process, the LNG is pumped into a cryogenic storage tank. These tanks are typically double-walled, with an outer wall of reinforced concrete lined with carbon steel and an inner wall of nickel steel. Between the two walls is insulation to prevent ambient air from warming the LNG. The LNG is stored in these tanks until a tanker is available to take the LNG to market. Storage tanks are sized based on the size of the tankers that will transport the LNG plus additional capacity to allow for scheduling flexibility and handling of plant outages. Many facilities include multiple tanks with the total capacity typically sized for twice the size of the expected tanker capacity so that up to two tankers worth of LNG can be stored at one time. Current tank sizes range from 36,000 m^3 to 188,000 m^3 with typical tanks sized in the 136,000 to 148,000 m^3 range.

Ship Loading Facilities

Ship loading facilities include the berth where the LNG tanker docks, a jetty which is a wall built out into the water, an insulated pipeline from the tanks to the berth, and rigid loading arms. After an empty tanker docks in the berth, the LNG is loaded onto the tanker through insulated pipes that are attached to the tanker by rigid loading arms. Once the tanker is filled, the pipes are disconnected, the loading arms are swung away from the ship, and the tanker is ready to sail.

Liquefaction Plant Costs

Capital Costs

The capital cost of a liquefaction plant is a critical component of the overall cost of an LNG delivery chain. In fact, total costs of a facility can run as high as $4 billion. The initial liquefaction plants were small in size compared to those being built today, with no trains over 2 mtpa built until the 1990s. As the LNG trade became more than a small niche market, plant owners began looking for ways to lower costs. One key was to take advantage of economies of scale by building larger facilities. As you can see from the chart on the left, the cost of liquefaction plants has fluctuated over time. Construction costs came down in the 1990s and early 2000s due to a number of influences

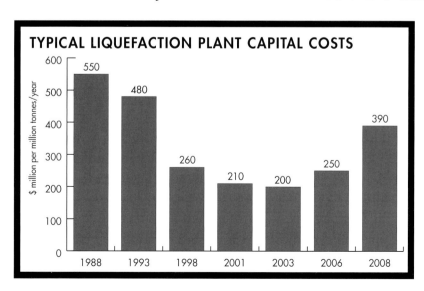

including economies of scale; supplier competition; advancements in organizational learning, research and development; and project management techniques. But by 2005, costs began to escalate rapidly as worldwide demand for materials such as steel, nickel and concrete rose rapidly. Also climbing were costs for engineering contractors, engineers and skilled laborers due to a boom in building driven by rapidly growing Asian economies. As of early 2010, it was uncertain whether the economic slowdown would again bring down costs or whether they would remain high.

Variable Costs

Ongoing costs to operate a liquefaction unit are also an important factor in the overall cost of liquefaction. Important factors include use of natural gas as fuel in the liquefaction plant, taxes paid to the local government and general operating and maintenance (O&M) costs. A typical liquefaction unit might use 11% of the plant's input gas as fuel. If we assume a fuel cost of $0.75/Mcf (current supply costs range from $0.55 to about $1/Mcf) then the operating cost associated with use of fuel is approximately $0.08/Mcf. Taxes will vary depending on where the facility is located but might be on the order of $0.15/Mcf and O&M costs are typically about $0.10/Mcf. The resulting overall variable cost of liquefaction is then about $0.33/Mcf.

EXAMPLE OF LIQUEFACTION COSTS	
Total plant capital cost	$2.4 billion
Plant capacity	5 mtpa (238 Bcf/year)
Utilization rate	90%
Annual cost of capital	$310 million
Per Mcf cost of capital	$1.44/Mcf
Fuel	$0.08/Mcf
Taxes	$0.15/Mcf
Operating costs	$0.10/Mcf
Total cost of liquefaction	$1.77/Mcf

Plant capital cost includes interest during construction.

Liquefaction Infrastructure

Existing Plants

As of early 2010, liquefaction plants were operating in 16 countries at 26 different sites. Total production capacity was approximately 230 mpta worldwide. Actual production was at about 80% of full capacity. The table on page 31 lists the exporting countries along with the amount of LNG they exported in 2008. A complete list of worldwide liquefaction terminals is included in Appendix D.

LIQUEFACTION MARKET SHARE (2008)		
Country	Volume (million tonnes)	Market Share
Qatar	28.77	17.5%
Malaysia	21.32	13.0%
Indonesia	19.47	11.9%
Algeria	15.86	9.7%
Nigeria	14.89	9.1%
Australia	14.68	8.9%
Trinidad and Tobago	12.59	7.7%
Egypt	10.20	6.2%
Oman	7.90	4.8%
Brunei	6.67	4.1%
United Arab Emirates	5.47	3.3%
Equatorial Guinea	3.76	2.3%
Norway	1.59	1.0%
United States	0.70	0.4%
Libya	0.38	0.2%

Based on annual exports listed in *BP Statistical Review of World Energy 2009*.

Historically, a typical LNG liquefaction plant has consisted of between one and three process trains, though some plants have used as many as six. In simple terms, a train can be viewed as a standalone liquefaction unit (i.e., it is possible to shut down one train without impacting the operation of other trains). Multiple trains add flexibility to plant design by allowing the operator to match the number of trains online to the amount of available gas. Today some facilities are being designed for greater flexibility within a single train, allowing for a reduction in the number of trains commonly required for new or expanded facilities.

The initial liquefaction plants built in the 1960s and 1970s consisted of multiple trains with lower capacities. For example, the first commercial LNG plant was constructed with three trains, each with a capacity of .37 mtpa. Five years later, the Kenai, Alaska plant[1] came online with two trains, each with a capacity of .70 mtpa.

The initial liquefaction design, which featured smaller and multiple trains per plant, was probably necessitated by a market whose primary focus was supply security – even at additional capital cost. The older projects were built with generous capacity margins and redundant design features to assure security of supply with the ability to meet contractual supply obligations. But beginning in the late 1990s, train size began to increase dramatically, and the common number of trains dropped to one or two per plant. Experience has allowed plant owners to decrease the design redundancy of their facilities which in turn has reduced the capital costs per train.

---

[1] The Kenai plant is sometimes referred to as a single train facility. Its design is actually a "two-in-one" configuration, making both a single train and a two train label correct.

SECTION THREE: LIQUEFACTION

Although demand for new liquefaction slowed from the mid-1980s through the first half of the 1990s, a new boom in demand began in the late 1990s and continues today. In the period from 2000 to 2010, over 115 mtpa of new liquefaction capacity was commissioned, representing a doubling in world capacity over the decade. The associated capital cost for these new plants was some $25 billion. An additional 68 mpta of liquefaction was under construction as of early 2010.

Proposed and Future Plants

It appears that growth in liquefaction will continue to be strong. Countries with excess gas supply exist in many regions around the globe and most are looking at whether LNG development could allow them to monetize these assets.

Much of the current construction of liquefaction capacity is in the Middle East, driven by Qatar's push to increase its position as the world leader in LNG production. Qatar commissioned a new 7.8 mtpa plant in 2009 and as of early 2010 had an additional 39 mtpa of capacity under construction, consisting of five more 7.8 mtpa "mega-trains." Also under construction in the Middle East was a 10.8 mtpa facility in Iran.

8.8 mtpa of capacity was under construction in the Pacific Basin as of early 2010. This includes the Pluto LNG facility in Australia and Peru LNG in South America. Meanwhile in the Atlantic Basin, 10 mtpa of capacity was under construction including the rebuild of Skikda Gl 1K in Algeria, Angola LNG, and Skangass in Norway. The Atlantic projects will add an additional 3 trains.

When current construction is complete, Angola, Iran, Peru, Russia, and Yemen will have joined the list of countries exporting LNG within a three-year time span. In addition to the projects under construction, there are liquefaction plants in the advanced planning stages in Nigeria and Australia, and additional potential projects in Algeria, Angola, Canada, Egypt, Equatorial Guinea, Indonesia, Libya, Papua New Guinea, Russia, Trinidad and Tobago, and Venezuela.

Key Issues

Key issues to watch are the development of new technology needed to accommodate offshore liquefaction terminals, sizing of liquefaction trains, market changes impacting the design of liquefaction, and environmental concerns. Throughout the world, much of the stranded gas under development exists offshore. Yet to date, all liquefaction facilities have been built onshore with close proximity to a safe harbor. Because large gas reserves exist offshore, liquefaction technology is currently being developed for offshore application. While offshore plants will have costs associated with building a platform that holds the liquefaction plant, they eliminate the need for land purchase, jetty facilities and compression, and pipeline to move gas to shore. They may also be easier to build than onshore facilities. Proponents of offshore projects currently in planning stages claim costs may be comparable or even lower than costs for onshore plants.

Similar to the debate between onshore and offshore facilities, there are differing approaches to train sizes. Some project developers believe that bigger trains will result in economies of scale driving down costs. Qatar recently completed one large 7.8 mpta train and has five more under construction. The success of these projects will be watched closely by many. An alternative viewpoint is represented by the small 0.3 mtpa Skangass project in Norway. This project is designed to take advantage of smaller gas fields, rapid construction (which ties up less capital) and fewer environmental impacts. Its size will allow smaller tankers to be used which opens the possibility of direct LNG sales to industrial customers. The developers of this project hope to take their concept elsewhere in the world if it proves successful.

The LNG marketplace is beginning to demand more flexibility in timing and amount of gas taken from liquefaction facilities. To accommodate these contractual terms, LNG liquefaction plants have to be able to reduce their output to match market demand, or find a ship and market available to purchase the spot load. This production flexibility is dependent upon plant design as discussed previously in this Section. While growth in this market is unquestionably favorable for the asset owner, the flexibility now required makes the business significantly more complicated.

In addition to volume flexibility, the evolving marketplace for spot sales impacts the quality requirements of gas produced from liquefaction. If a liquefaction facility has the ability to adjust the Btu content of the LNG as needed, more markets are available to that product. Thus facilities with quality adjustment capability will be more profitable in today's buyer's market.

While volume and product flexibility have significant impacts on profitability in today's LNG market, environmental concerns are also important. The Norwegian Snohvit plant completed in 2007 is the first example of a facility using electric motors instead of gas compression in order to reduce NO_x emissions. This facility will also remove CO_2 from the gas stream for reinjection into the producing field to further curtail greenhouse gas emissions. Such emphasis on environmental concerns is likely to be a trend for future plants.

What you will learn:

- How LNG tankers are constructed and operated

- Types of LNG tankers

- Typical shipping costs

- Characteristics of the LNG shipping fleet

- Key issues associated with shipping

SECTION FOUR: SHIPPING

Within the LNG delivery chain, shipping is the all-important conduit through which large volumes of LNG move from areas where natural gas is produced to areas where natural gas is consumed. While LNG can also be moved by truck and rail tanker car, the marine receipt and delivery of LNG is more common as it allows large quantities of LNG to be economically transported all over the world. Commercial shipping of LNG via marine tanker began in the 1960s with shipments from Algeria to the United Kingdom. It took 34 years for the LNG tanker fleet to number 100 active vessels. After an additional eight years that number was over 200. And in just three additional years, ending in 2008, the LNG tanker fleet launched its 300th ship. As of early 2010, over 330 ships were crossing the globe transporting LNG from producing countries to all the major consuming markets. In this Section we will explore the technology and costs associated with the specialized fleet of ships that safely and economically transports LNG across the globe. We will also discuss the existing and planned tanker fleet and explore key issues for the future of LNG shipping.

Ship Technology

LNG is transported in large tanker ships that are specially designed and built for safe transport of LNG. These tankers are double-hulled and carry an insulated containment system, or storage tank, that holds the LNG and keeps it cool. A typical LNG tanker is about 900 feet long, 140 feet wide, 36 feet in depth and has a draft (depth the ship sits in the water) of about 15 feet. This ship size is similar to an aircraft carrier. The average tanker carries from 125,000 to 200,000 m^3 of LNG at atmospheric pressure, which when regasified provides about 2.8 to 4.4 Bcf of natural gas. In recent years, ships with capacities as large as 266,000 m^3 have gone into service. The tankers are classified by capacity. Ships with capacities below 100,000 m^3 are called small, ships with capacities between 100,000 and 200,000 m^3 are called standard, ships with capacities between 200,000 and 217,000 m^3 are called Q-Flex, and ships with capacities above 250,000 m^3 are called Q-Max. A tanker typically travels at a speed of 15 to 20 knots (17 to 23 miles per hour).

SECTION FOUR: SHIPPING

While certain features of LNG tankers are similar to other liquid cargo carrying ships, special features make them quite unique and, as you will learn, expensive. These features include double hulls to safeguard against spills, cryogenic storage tanks designed to keep the cargo cold, vapor capture systems to safely remove any methane that returns to gaseous state, monitoring systems to ensure that the cargo remains safe, and specially designed loading and off-loading arms. Because of the potential for severe accidents associated with LNG, the design, construction, and operation of LNG tankers are all subject to strict certification requirements set by the International Maritime Organization (IMO). There are a number of key features that distinguish LNG tanker technology:

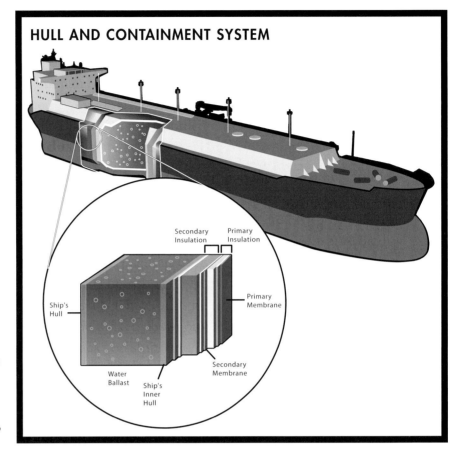

- The hull and containment system
- Vapor capture and cargo monitoring
- The ship's propulsion system
- Loading and unloading equipment

Each of these is discussed in detail in the following paragraphs.

The Hull and Containment System

As a line of defense against spills or leakage in the event of an accident, LNG tankers are designed with a double hull. The hulls are constructed of steel, with each layer having a thickness of about 3/4 of an inch. There is about 10 feet of space between the two hulls where water ballast can be held. For safety purposes, gas detectors are located between the two hulls so that an alarm is triggered in the event of a gas leak.

The product containment system is the most unique aspect of LNG transporting vessels. Because of the potential volatility of the cargo and the need to keep it cool, these systems are significantly more complex than storage systems for other types of liquid transport. In fact, as a result of the complexity involved, an LNG tanker costs about twice as much to build as a crude oil tanker of similar size. The containment system serves two functions – storage of the LNG and maintaining temperature so that the LNG stays in liquid state. The containment tanks function somewhat like a huge thermos bottle, with layers of insulation keeping atmospheric temperature from warming the cargo. While warming is kept to a minimum by insulation, some of the LNG will revert to a gaseous state due to motion or slosh of the cryogenic liquid. This vaporization of the LNG is called boil-off. Because vaporization results in cooling, it counteracts the small amount of heat leaking in through the insulation, thus maintaining an equilibrium that keeps the bulk of the cargo in liquid state.

Different types of containment systems are used on different LNG vessels. The selection of the cargo containment system is primarily governed by the expected trade application, the routes the vessel will serve and cost considerations. The two main types of LNG containment systems currently in use are Moss sphere tanks and membrane tanks. About half of the current LNG fleet uses Moss sphere tanks. These spherical vessels are self-contained, structurally independent tanks set into the deck of the tanker with roughly half of the tank below deck and the other half above. Each containment tank is double-walled with both an insulating layer and a vapor recovery layer between the inner and outer storage tank walls. Tank walls are typically built of an aluminum alloy and the preferred insulation is plastic foam. A typical Moss sphere tanker has four to six separate tanks.

Most of the rest of the current fleet and the vast majority of the new orders use membrane tanks. Membrane tanks are double-walled storage containers designed to fill the space below deck and to contour to the ships' hull (see illustration on page 36). Unlike sphere tanks which are self-supporting, membrane tanks are built up from the ship's hull. Inner membrane walls are built either of Invar (a steel alloy consisting of 36% nickel and 64% iron) which will not expand under temperature changes or of stainless steel with corrugation to allow for thermal expansion. Depending on the ship design the outer membrane may also be built of Invar or may be built of an aluminum-glass fiber called Triplex. Reinforced plastic foam or perlite (a naturally occurring siliceous rock that has strong insulating characteristics) is used for insulation both between the two membranes and between the outer membrane and the ship hull. Because the tanks use more of the below deck space for storage than the Moss sphere design, membrane tanks allow for additional storage area with less wind drag.

A third design uses prismatic shaped tanks that are self-supporting and sit within the hull of the tanker. These tanks were originally built to store LNG in the retrofitted cargo ships initially used to transport LNG during the 1960s. Although a few of these ships are still in use, this design never gained popularity for ships constructed since the 1960s. However, current renewed interest in this design may result in future ships being built with prismatic tanks.

Many new containment system variations have been proposed and approved in principle by the American Bureau of Shipping (ABS), one of the world's leading ship classification societies. However, many ship builders are unwilling to change established designs. Possible barriers to change include the time-consuming and expensive nature of the approval or certification proces, the potential for costly revision of construction facilties and procedures such as workforce re-training, and existing LNG import and export terminal limitations in accepting tankers outside a certain design range. With the increased need for added flexibility in load sizes, deliveries and routes, innovative designs may gain popularity in the future.

Vapor Capture and Cargo Monitoring

Since LNG is a cryogenic liquid and the storage tanks are well insulated, refrigeration is not required to maintain its liquid state at –260 Fahrenheit. However, the increased pressure caused by boil-off can result in cargo warming. Thus pressure maintenance is a critical factor in keeping the LNG from warming up, expanding and vaporizing. To prevent pressure rise, boil-off is captured by a vapor recovery system. Boil-off, which is basically vaporized LNG, can be used as ship fuel, can be reliquefied and returned to tank storage, or can be vented to the atmosphere to safely relieve the pressure in the tank. Current tankers use the majority of boil-off as a fuel for the propulsion system. For safety reasons, a secondary vapor removal system is required which acts as an overpressure relief valve that will vent vapor to the atmosphere in the event tank pressures rise above safe levels. Some newer tankers are now being designed to use fuel other than natural gas for propulsion. These may require an on-board reliquefaction plant using cooling by nitrogen to return boil-off to liquid state.

Propulsion

The LNG marine transportation sector is the last of the ocean-based fleets using steam as the main type of propulsion system. When the first LNG carriers were built in the 1960s, some 50% of the world's merchant ships used steam propulsion. Since LNG boil-off gas was readily available for fuel, it made sense to utilize steam propulsion for LNG carriers. The gas could simply be burned in a steam boiler and used to power the ship. Even the design speed of the early ships was, in part, chosen to balance the power requirement with the expected amount of boil-off.

Most LNG tankers currently depend on boil-off as a fuel for propulsion. To accomplish this, the boil-off is burned in a boiler to create steam. The steam, in turn, spins steam turbines which rotate the drive shaft to propel the ship. Most LNG tankers in service today use between 0.15% and 0.25% of their LNG cargo per day as fuel for the average 480-mile daily journey. Thus the length of shipping time has a direct impact on the amount of LNG ultimately delivered to the customer as well as the economics of the voyage.

Two alternate propulsion systems have gained favor in recent years by using fuel sources that are cheaper than LNG. They are the Dual Fuel Diesel Electric (DFDE) system and the low speed diesel system with reliquefaction (DRL). The DFDE system burns the boil-off gas and marine diesel in dual fuel diesel engines. The engines drive generators to produce electricity for the electric motors driving the ship. With the DRL system, the engines burn cheaper heavy fuel oil for ship propulsion. This system completely separates the propulsion system from the cargo handling system. All boil-off gas is reliquefied and returned to the cargo tanks.

Just as with containment systems, many new propulsion systems have been proposed and modeled and are currently under consideration for new ships. These include a more efficient steam turbine; a slow-speed diesel with a fixed-pitch propeller and reliquefaction; a slow-speed diesel with a controllable-pitch propeller, power take-off and reliquefaction; a medium-speed diesel with single fuel (HFO) and reliquefaction; a medium-speed diesel with dual fuels (boil-off gas and diesel); a medium-speed diesel with a mechanical drive; a medium-speed diesel with an electric drive; a gas turbine with a mechanical drive; and a gas turbine with an electric drive. Each type of propulsion system has advantages for various applications. As the world of LNG continues to evolve, more propulsion systems are likely to move from model to production.

SECTION FOUR: SHIPPING

Loading and Unloading

LNG ships load and unload product from a series of arms located on the center port side of the tanker which are designed for the rapid loading and unloading of LNG. An average tanker can be loaded or unloaded in approximately ten to twelve hours. With the extra time required to dock the ship, connect the discharge lines and turn the ship for its journey back to sea, the average tanker port time is 48 hours.

The arm configuration typically includes three lines – two of which carry LNG into the storage tank at the terminal and a third that returns any natural gas that has vaporized during the process. The vaporized natural gas will be kept on-board the ship for use as fuel during the return trip. The lines that carry LNG must be designed to handle the cold temperatures associated with LNG and are typically made of stainless steel. Expansion loops and bellows are built into the pipes to allow for contraction when the pipe comes in contact with the cold LNG. A ship-to-shore emergency shut-down system with automatic shut-off valves can stop the ship's unloading pumps and close flow valves both on the ship and the shore within 20 to 30 seconds in an emergency. Quick-release couplings automatically disconnect the unloading arms upon shut-down. Most LNG tankers retain a small portion of LNG in their storage tanks to keep them cool during their return trip as well as for use as additional return fuel. The LNG tank cooling portion, or heel, is usually less than 5% of the cargo capacity.

As more terminals are built offshore, locations are chosen with increasingly severe conditions, and the number of ship-to-ship transfers increases, design changes will be necessary to allow the safe transfer of LNG. Newly designed loading arms have been developed to enable the transfer of LNG at offshore and exposed locations in a side-by-side configuration as well as a bow configuration. The new generation side-by-side LNG loading arms have a specially developed targeting system that enables the safe connection and disconnection of the arms to the LNG carrier's manifold in more dynamic conditions caused by wave motions. These side-by-side LNG transfer applications are highly engineered to adapt to all six types of relative sea movement for both vessels. This new technology has already achieved significant commercial success. When the environmental conditions for offloading become too severe, a more expensive option called tandem mooring (similar to those used offshore for crude oil) is the best option. This loading arm development is based on the soft yoke mooring system already in use in the crude oil business. LNG transfer occurs either by flexible cryogenic hose or specifically designed loading arms.

Ship Certification

Due to the possibility of catastrophic incidents associated with LNG tankers, all ships must be certified by the IMO. In addition, ships transporting LNG in U.S. waters must meet more stringent U.S. Coast Guard requirements. The LNG ship building process is overseen or "registered" by a classification society (e.g., Lloyd's Registry), which is an organization whose function is to study, audit and certify the technical aspects involved in shipbuilding – from materials selection and design through construction techniques to final testing and ship maintenance. Every time a change in ship design occurs, the change must be certified and registered before the tanker can operate in LNG transport service. The classification society actively participates in industry modeling and approval of all proposed changes to standard specifications (e.g., tanker size, propulsion system type, and loading arm design and location). Because of these strict construction standards and oversight, there are now only 14 shipyards in the world actively building LNG tankers. While LNG tankers were once built in the U.S., no U.S. shipyard is currently certified to build them.

Shipping Costs

Capital Costs

The cost of LNG transport vessels has evolved substantially over time. During the first building spree in the 1970s, ships were expensive due to lack of construction experience and ever increasing size. But as with most products, experience brings efficiency. By the beginning of the 1980s, most new LNG tankers built were in the 125,000 to 138,000 m^3 size range with an average price tag of $250 million. As the LNG shipping industry entered a second building spree in the 1990s, tanker prices had reached an all-time high of $285 million. But by the end of the decade, expansion of shipyards in Asia coupled with world recession helped bring down the cost of LNG vessels by as much as 40%. With fewer orders for any type of ships, the yards capable of building LNG tankers began competing for construction contracts. And by 1999, tanker prices were as low as $155 million. Since that time, prices for ships in sizes up to 145,000 m^3 have crept up and prices of recently delivered ships of this size now range from $151 to $210 million. New cutting edge vessels in the 215,000 to 260,000 m^3 size range are currently priced between $215 and $290 million.

While current ship costs on a per unit basis are well below those seen in the 1980s, several factors suggest that prices are in a state of flux. While 2008 was a record year with 54 new vessels delivered, the volume delivered drop to 38 in 2009. China's entrance into the LNG shipbuilding foray suggests renewed competition among shipbuilders for new orders. This competition combined with reduced demand due to a worldwide recession may put downward price pressure on new vessels built in the near future. However, material prices for steel, nickel and aluminum continue to trade at a higher level than in past decades. While some decline has recently occurred, the higher material prices will be passed along to ship buyers. Finally, labor costs have risen some 11% from 2007.

In calculating the development cost of the LNG delivery chain, we must also consider that within any single chain, multiple ships are required if the chain is to function at maximum efficiency. Due to distances involved in shipping, the available ship sizes, and the liquefaction train sizes needed to produce LNG economically, more than one tanker is required to continuously move LNG to market. On average three to seven ships are required for most LNG delivery chains. So even though the cost of a single ship seems small when compared to other assets in the delivery chain, the need for multiple ships pushes the capital investment into the $500 million to $1 billion range. The sheer size of the shipping investment acts as a barrier to entry for all but the largest companies.

EXAMPLE OF SHIPPING COSTS	
Total ship capital cost	$180 million
Ship capacity	3.0 Bcf/tanker
Utilization rate	90%
Annual cost of capital	$23 million
Per Mcf cost of capital	$0.61/Mcf
Fuel	$0.35/Mcf
Operating costs	$0.15/Mcf
Total cost of shipping	$1.11/Mcf

Note that these costs will vary significantly depending on how far the LNG is transported and the cost of fuel used for propulsion.

Variable Costs

Of course, capital costs are only one piece of the cost of shipping. Once an LNG vessel is in service, there are also operating and maintenance expenses to be considered. Important factors include the cost of fuel for propulsion, administrative and general expenses (including costs for the crew, taxes, insurance, and O&M) plus port costs. Typical costs for shipping will vary depending on how far the LNG is transported, the type of vessel used and the price associated with the cost of the boil-off or diesel fuel. Typical variable costs are on the order of $0.01 to $0.02/Mcf per day of shipping.

Several factors suggest these variable costs are rising. First, with more vessels on the water, a notable shortage of trained officers has led to a sharp increase in wages. Along with this cost increase are the increases in O&M, especially lube oil costs due to higher crude prices, and higher insurance rates reflecting the increase in risks associated with new technology and less seasoned crews.

The LNG Fleet

The Existing Fleet

As you might imagine, the current fleet of LNG tankers has changed dramatically from the initial ships that were launched in the 1960s. The most striking difference is capacity. The first ships moved what we would now consider very small volumes – 25,000 to 27,000 m³. The first Moss sphere and membrane LNG tankers were launched in the early 1970s beginning a new era of larger ships with storage volumes of 70,000 to 87,000 m³. The first ships to break the 100,000 m³ barrier were launched in 1976. And today, the average tanker has a capacity of 125,000 to 200,000 m³. The largest tanker in service is capable of hauling 266,000 m³.

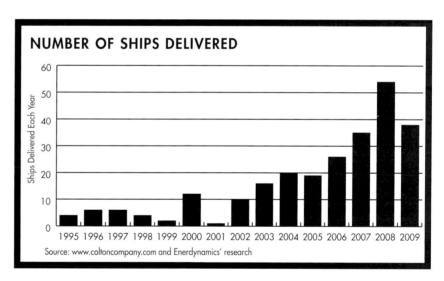

As of early 2010 there were over 330 LNG ships actively transporting LNG around the world with an additional 38 ships under construction or on order. The existing fleet was built in two waves. The first flurry of building occurred in the 1970s with the fleet reaching 50 vessels. The next big tanker boom began in 1993 and continues today. For the three years from 2002 through 2004, the fleet grew by 44 new ships, as many as were built in the first 15 years of the business. In 2004, 20 new ships were delivered including the first dual-fuel tanker and the first floating regasification and storage tanker (Excelerate's Energy Bridge™ Regasification Vessel). In 2008, a record 54 ships were delivered including the first from a Chinese shipyard. It is unlikely that this record will fall anytime soon given the change in economic climate and the corresponding demand for global gas, but construction of new ships currently continues at a lower rate.

In addition to new ships, this decade is also likely to see the first wave of ship retirements. In fact, five smaller ships were scrapped in 2007 and 2008. The age of the LNG fleet will become increasingly important over the next few years as about 34% of the existing fleet is greater than ten years old and 23% of the fleet is greater than 20 years old. While a well-maintained vessel can easily last 40 or more years, some of the older ships are scheduled for retirement each year for the next ten years. Over 40 of the ships on order are replacement vessels for these retiring ships.

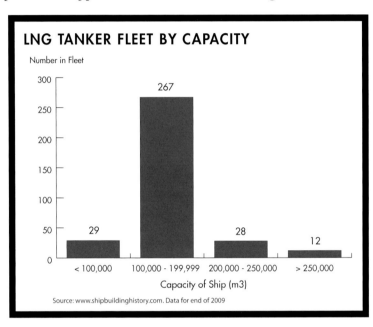

Future Fleets

LNG tankers are getting significantly larger as the worldwide demand for LNG increases. The largest vessels are designed to match the larger liquefaction trains and longer trade routes now common in the industry. Larger ship capacities also help to reduce the per unit cost of LNG transportation, making longer distance transport more economic. Unfortunately, the larger ship sizes do not come without challenges. The Q-Flex ships require a deepwater port of 40 feet along with enough space for turning the ship around. Not all existing receipt terminals can accommodate these requirements. And the larger Q-Max ships will face even greater restrictions. Historically, tankers were built for and dedicated to a single liquefaction plant and a single delivery terminal. But as the LNG business becomes more flexible, vessels must have the option to move between multiple receipt and delivery points. Thus, ship size can restrict the opportunities available to maximize margin from spot loads or physical swaps unless ship-to-ship transfers are utilized. Even with the average ship size today, routes are mostly restricted to either the Atlantic or Pacific basin due to the inability of LNG tankers to fit through the Panama Canal and the added expense of traveling around South America. With the Canal expansion slated to be completed in 2010, we may see more vessels crossing between the two markets.

The most important changes for the future of shipping involve innovative new technologies designed to increase efficiency and profit margins. These include new containment concepts, flexible loading arms, new or dual propulsion systems, and specially built ships that include onboard liquefaction and regasification. As you have learned, each change must be certified by a classification society prior to commissioning the vessel. The propulsion system changes are the easiest to certify since the technology has been used elsewhere, not just in LNG service. The changes requiring more lead time are generally new concepts using unproven technology such as off-loading methods.

Today, all LNG ships use mid-ship loading and off-loading methods. This design works well for terminals located onshore in calm waters. But given the resistance to building new onshore LNG regasification terminals, many of the proposed terminals are being sited offshore. These offshore terminals can be located in shallow or deep water, can be floating or permanently anchored to the ocean floor, and can be atop existing offshore platforms or on floating LNG tankers. With an increase in wave height and movement between the terminal and the tanker (relative to docking in an onshore port), mid-ship off-loading becomes more risky. New loading arms and docking systems have been designed to compensate for the more challenging offshore conditions. To date, mock-up prototypes of the new arm designs have been built and tested, but the ships utilizing these new designs have been ordered but not yet delivered.

Most current LNG tankers use steam turbine propulsion systems. While this technology is proven, it is inefficient compared with other means of propulsion. The cost of the gas consumed coupled with higher emissions may make this technology less desirable in the future. Several other propulsion systems have been studied including gas turbine drives, internal combustion engines using gasoline, diesel, or CNG (compressed natural gas), electric engines, and electric/diesel combination drives. All of these systems can be less expensive to operate than the steam-driven method. An additional benefit is that these systems result in incremental space for LNG storage because the fuel can be stored on deck and less space may be required for the engines themselves. They can also result in more cargo being delivered by each ship since the boil-off can be cooled for reinjection into the storage tanks. In recent years, ships using diesel, dual electric/diesel and fuel oil systems have been built and commissioned.

Excelerate's Energy Bridge™ Regasification Vessel also shows great potential to revolutionize the LNG shipping industry. The tanker contains its own regasification equipment and can off-load into an offshore pipeline using a specialized buoy. It also has the flexibility to off-load natural gas directly to a land-based pipeline system or LNG to any standard terminal.

Samsung Heavy Industries (SHI) has also begun production of a concept that could revolutionize the upstream end of the value chain. The LNG-FPSO (floating production, storage and offloading) vessel developed by SHI is specially designed for the commercialization of small and medium-sized marine gas fields scattered worldwide in around 2,400 sites. A contract was recently signed for an LNG-FPSO vessel that will be built using prismatic storage tanks with capacities of 210,000 m^3 of LNG storage, a liquefaction plant on deck, and traditional side-by-side offloading. These floating liquefaction plants use lower tech liquefaction concepts but offer the location flexibility to monetize even small fields. Several other companies such as Shell, Mustang, CB&I, and Teekay are also pursuing this technology.

4 Key Issues

Key issues to watch are ship technology changes necessary to accommodate offshore terminals and market changes that impact the cost of shipping. Also critical are issues associated with safety and security, which will be covered in Section Six.

Throughout the world, resistance to building onshore terminals is growing. As security issues take center stage, the answer may lie in offshore facilities. As of 2010, five offshore terminals were in service worldwide, with more under construction or proposed. While potentially more palatable from a security standpoint, offshore terminals bring technology challenges. While offshore movement of other commodities has occurred for decades, the offshore option is relatively new for both LNG receipt terminals and LNG transport vessels. Retrofitting existing LNG tankers to deliver to offshore terminals presents challenges to the shipping industry and could become a bottleneck to the efficient movement of LNG if use of offshore terminals expands. Meanwhile delivery of the first ships for offshore delivery using the Energy Bridge™ system has occurred, and if the technology proves successful we can expect to see more interest in ships with onboard regasification technology. The first delivery of floating liquefaction ships is expected in 2010. If this proves successful, it too could change the face of shipping.

Of course, there will always be a desire to reduce shipping costs. Costs are currently being driven down by construction of larger ships, which reduces the per unit costs of long-haul transport. As discussed earlier in the Section, the next key area for cost reduction may be the propulsion systems, which also affect the primary environmental issue for LNG tankers – emissions during transport and in port. This concern may lead to further use of diesel or electric power propulsion.

What you will learn:

- How LNG is regasified

- The steps in the regasification process

- Typical costs of regasification

- Where regasification terminals exist today and where new terminals have been proposed

- Key issues associated with regasification

SECTION FIVE: REGASIFICATION

You have now learned about two important components of the LNG delivery chain: liquefaction and shipping. The final step is regasification, in which the LNG is returned to its original gaseous form and then injected into the domestic pipeline grid for delivery to customers. Regasification usually occurs in an onshore terminal that includes docking facilities for an LNG tanker, one or more storage tanks to hold the LNG until regasification capacity is available, and a regasification plant. However, in some cases it is regasified offshore and transported onshore by an undersea pipeline. LNG is converted back to natural gas by carefully warming the liquid until it vaporizes. It can then be injected into a pipeline and co-mingled with other natural gas supplies for delivery to the consumer. In this Section we will explore the technology and costs associated with the regasification process. We will also discuss both existing and planned regasification infrastructure around the world and will explore key issues for the future of regasification.

Regasification Technology

The basic steps in the regasification process are:

1. Berthing and unloading of the LNG tanker
2. Storage of LNG
3. Vaporization
4. Delivery into the pipeline grid

The process is slightly different for offshore regasification. Each step is discussed in detail in the following paragraphs.

Berthing and Unloading

Today, the vast majority of LNG is unloaded at onshore terminals. To do this, the tanker is parked and moored at a berth alongside the LNG terminal. The water in the berth must be deep enough to accommodate LNG tankers which usually require a depth of 40 feet or more. Discharge or unloading lines are then attached mid-ship to the LNG tanker's discharge valves. The discharge lines rest on a trestle built from the berth to the onshore storage tanks that protects and stabilizes them. The discharge system includes high volume pumps to accomplish the movement of the LNG from the ship to the shore. The marine facilities for each onshore regasification facility are site specific and require custom design to fit each terminal.

Storage

Each regasification facility contains one or more specialized, full containment storage tanks capable of holding a minimum of one shipload of LNG. Onshore storage tanks are not only a holding place for LNG, but can also be used as blending facilities to adjust the heating content by mixing supplies from multiple shiploads of LNG. Typical tank sizes range from 55,000 to 180,000 m^3, but economies of scale have resulted in larger tanks being built in recent years, with 200,000 m^3 tanks now commonly specified where space permits. Many terminals install multiple tanks to obtain the desired storage capacity. A facility's storage capacity depends on a number of factors. Tanks are designed to allow for the largest LNG tanker possible to offload its full capacity plus additional capacity to allow LNG from an earlier cargo to be held in the event that multiple cargos are available before the vaporization facility is able to regasify the earlier cargo. If the terminal is in a region where market demand fluctuates, additional storage capacity may be built so that plant output can be matched to market needs, with the LNG stored in the tank until consumers require the gas.

Several types of LNG storage tanks are used throughout the world today. The most common are above ground tanks which include:

- Single containment tanks which are doubled walled (9% nickel inner tank, carbon steel outer tank).

- Double containment tanks with primary and secondary tanks (9% nickel inner tank, carbon steel outer tank with a carbon steel roof, surrounded by free standing pre-stressed concrete wall).

- Full containment tanks with primary and secondary tanks that are hardened to withstand impacts from missiles or flying objects (9% nickel inner tank, pre-stressed concrete outer tank with carbon steel liner, concrete roof).

The difference between the types of tank has to do with the level of protection against spillage and projectiles built into the design. In all designs the inner tank is made of

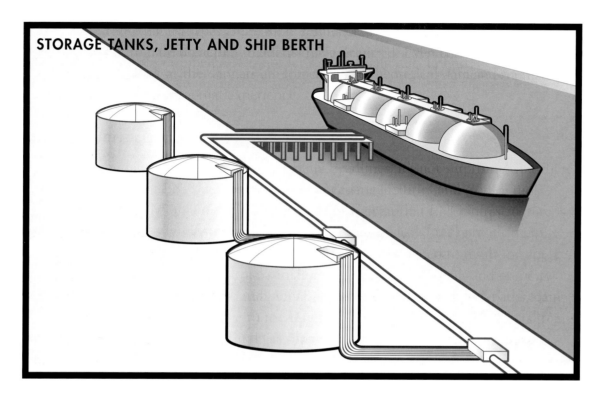

steel consisting of 9% nickel. A single containment tank has only a carbon steel outer tank surrounding the inner tank. The double containment tank adds the protection of a steel roof and a concrete wall. If a leak were to occur, the concrete wall would prevent the LNG from spreading and thus would limit the vaporization and size of an LNG pool. The full containment tanks add the protection of a concrete roof and full concrete outer tank designed to withstand impacts from missiles or flying objects. Most new storage tanks are constructed with full containment for safety and security.

Tanks can also be built below-ground or partially below-ground. Buried tanks are usually built using a design called a membrane tank. This type of tank has a pre-stressed concrete outer tank, a lining of polyurethane foam insulation, and a thin steel inner-tank called a membrane layer. Partially below-ground tanks are similar in design to full containment tanks. While below-ground or partially below-ground tanks are considered safer than above-ground tanks, they are also more expensive to construct so their use is less common than above-ground tanks.

Since the inner tank has direct contact with the LNG, the specialized steel used must be able to withstand extreme temperatures. To accomplish this, the nickel steel inner tank is insulated with a non-flammable type of insulation such as perlite. A vacuum system is also employed so that any vapors that might escape from an inner tank weld

SECTION FIVE: REGASIFICATION

or crack are recovered for safe handling. All penetrations through the tank for vapor management and for injecting/removing the LNG are through the roof thus reducing the risk of leaks. Fire and vapor detection systems are used throughout the storage facility so that any leaks or fires can be quickly detected and automatic fire-suppression response can be triggered promptly. Tanks are placed in a walled and bermed impoundment system that will collect and drain spilled LNG in the event of a tank failure. Normally tank impoundments are designed to handle a volume of at least 110% of the tank volume.

The storage tanks are generally the item requiring the longest lead-time to construct (typically two to three years). ExxonMobil introduced modular tanks in 2004 to address both issues. These scalable, modular tanks are constructed in shipyards and then barged to the LNG terminal. If modular tanks prove to reduce costs and construction time, they may well be the wave of the future.

Vaporization

The third step in the regasification process is vaporization. LNG receiving terminals typically use either an open rack vaporizer (ORV) or a submerged combustion vaporizer (SCV) to convert the liquefied gas back to a gaseous state. Other types of vaporizers include ambient air-heater vaporizers, combined heat and power units with gas-fired vaporizers, and shell and tube vaporizers. These are all much less common and are not discussed here.

ORVs are the most commonly found vaporizers and use seawater at ambient temperature as their source of heat. The LNG is vaporized using a heat exchanger which warms the LNG by passing it through radiator-like rows of tubes that are flushed with seawater. After the water is used to warm the LNG, it is collected and returned to the sea. Besides the ORV unit itself, required equipment includes large diameter intake and discharge pipes, pumping equipment and water treating facilities. The ORV is made of aluminum to handle the extreme temperatures, and the rows of tubes are coated in zinc to resist corrosion from seawater. The water is chlorinated to protect the surface of the tube panel and any inside piping from algae growth. Water quality and quantity are critical to successful operation of the ORV system. The water must contain no heavy metals and be low in solids. Because of the vast quantity of water required – from 18,000 to 65,000 m^3 per hour – the amount of sea life destroyed by mechanical intake or the chemically treated water can have an ecological impact. In addition, since the millions of gallons of seawater are returned at 5 to 12 degrees cooler than the ocean's ambient temperature, there is the potential for environmental impact from changing the natural temperature of the seawater around the facility.

The SCV vaporizes LNG contained in stainless steel tubes in a submerged warm water bath. A combustion burner fueled by natural gas provides the necessary heat to warm the water bath. The fuel source is usually low-pressure gas from facility boil-off. The water bath of an SCV uses significantly less water than the ORV since the water is contained and reused. Nevertheless, due to chemical reactions during the vaporization process, the water does require treatment before disposal. But since water is not continually being returned to the sea, SCVs are generally considered to be more environmentally friendly than ORVs, and most new North American terminals are using them to limit impact. Because of fewer equipment requirements, less space is needed to build an SCV. However, the increased cost of fuel (approximately 1.5 to 2.5% of the LNG received) offsets most of the capital savings.

Delivery into the Pipeline Grid

Before the gas can be delivered into the pipeline grid it must match pipeline grid specifications for temperature, pressure and composition. Temperature is determined by the regasification process and pressure can be adjusted through pressure regulators. If the gas quality is not within pipeline tariff standards, additional measures must be

---

LNG AND BTU CONTENT

Btu content is a measure of the energy contained within a specific volume of natural gas. Unfortunately, gas from different supply regions will naturally have varying Btu contents. Btu content can be adjusted during processing by leaving more or less of the heavier hydrocarbons (propane, butane, ethane) in the natural gas stream.

Adjusting for Btu content is important because different regions of the world traditionally use natural gas with different Btu contents. Because of this, consumer appliances must be designed with a specific Btu content in mind. Appliances from Japan will not work properly in the U.S. and vice-versa since we operate our gas systems with different standard Btu content. To further complicate the issue, as LNG boils off the concentration of heavy hydrocarbons gets higher, resulting in higher Btu content the further the LNG is transported. In a world of spot trading of LNG cargos, the liquefaction plant cannot always be designed and/or operated to ensure that LNG cargos will have the correct Btu content to match the ultimate market. Thus the ability to adjust the Btu content at the regasification terminal is becoming increasingly important. Both U.S. and European regulatory agencies are working to develop standards for gas interchangeability that will allow more flexibility in trading and delivering LNG cargos to multiple locations.

taken to bring the gas up to marketability standards. The most common problem is that the Btu content of the regasified LNG may not match the Btu content requirement of the pipeline. In some cases this can be handled by blending the regasified LNG with natural gas from other sources. If this is not possible, it is then necessary to condition the gas.

There are three common ways to adjust Btu content prior to send-out: fractionation, injecting inert gas such as nitrogen and injecting compressed air. Fractionation uses traditional cryogenic gas processing techniques to remove ethane, propane, butanes, and heavier hydrocarbons in liquid form from the gas stream. To do this, cooling and pressure are used to mechanically separate components in a similar manner to the way in which they are removed in the liquefaction process (see discussion in Section Three). Facilities to perform fractionation are typically available only if the LNG is delivered to a region with gas production such as the Gulf of Mexico in the U.S. If such facilities are not available, another method must be used.

Nitrogen or air injection can also be used to dilute the Btu content in a given volume of gas. Since nitrogen is an inert gas, it simply takes up space in the gas. Compressed air, while more economical, adds compounds and elements to the gas stream that could be problematic. However, since LNG is so clean from contaminants, air injection is often an acceptable method for reducing Btu content while remaining within specifications for other contaminants.

Offshore Regasification Technology

While most regasification facilities are located onshore, there has recently been development of multiple offshore facilities. These offer the advantage of avoiding local safety and security concerns and can often be brought into service more quickly than onshore terminals. The first offshore LNG receiving facility (the Gulf Gateway Deepwater Port in the U.S.) went into service in 2005. As of early 2010, there were six offshore facilities in service including two each in the U.S. and Brazil, and one each in Argentina and Italy. Technologies for offshore terminals are further discussed later in this Section. The vaporization technology used in an offshore terminal is similar to that used onshore and the choice of which type to use is usually driven by environmental concerns.

Onshore Regasification Plant Costs

Capital Costs

Onshore terminal capital costs can be considered in three segments – marine facilities, storage and regasification. Capital costs for an LNG terminal can vary significantly since each terminal is designed for site-specific conditions and markets. And as of early 2010, there was significant uncertainty in future materials and labor costs. Both escalated rapidly between 2005 and 2008 due to worldwide demand for materials and a lack of engineering and construction labor given a large number of terminal projects either under construction or in engineering. It is uncertain whether the economic downturn in 2009 will result in cost reductions.

Major cost variables for marine facilities include the need for a breakwater, dredging to accommodate the deep-hulled tankers and the length of the trestle. A marine facility requiring breakwaters, dredging and/or a long approach trestle may cost as much as $300 million.

Storage tanks represent the largest single piece of equipment needed in an onshore LNG terminal. Facility estimates will generally include at least enough storage to accommodate the volume from one to two tankers. Many existing terminals have added storage capacity over the last five years and now have a minimum of three times the storage necessary to off-load the largest tanker scheduled for the facility. A 160,000 m^3 full containment storage tank is estimated to cost $100 million or more. Thus if the facility is being constructed to handle 145,000 m^3 ships, the facility may be designed for three tanks at a total cost of up to $500 million.

A regasification terminal would characteristically include a dozen or more vaporizers, plus intake structures, pumps, piping, and the power plant. Total costs for vaporization

		PROPOSED FACILITY COSTS			
Terminal Name	**No. of berths**	**Storage**	**Vaporization**	**Estimated Cost**	**Year Completed**
Sabine Pass	2	3 x 160,000 m^3	2.6 Bcf/d	$1.4 billion	2008
Gulf LNG	1	2 x 160,000 m^3	1.3 Bcf/d	$1.1 billion	2011*
Cameron LNG	2	3 x 160,000 m^3	1.5 Bcf/d	$840 million	2009

*Planned completion date as of January, 2010.

equipment would typically be around $80 million for ORV technology or $50 million for SCV technology, assuming a 1Bcf/day plant. For both onshore and offshore terminals, additional costs may be incurred if the Btu content of the gas must be adjusted. Costs for fractionation, or nitrogen or compressed air injection equipment range from $30 to $60 million. The total cost of a single berth onshore terminal with two storage tanks and 1 Bcf/d output is approximately $1 billion.

Operating Costs

Ongoing operating costs for regasification include administrative costs, O&M, energy for pumps and compressors, and if SCVs are being used, fuel for heating the water. SCVs typically use about 1.5% of the vaporized natural gas as fuel, significantly increasing the variable cost of operation when this technology is used. Typical operating costs excluding fuel for SCVs are generally about $0.08/Mcf. The cost of fuel for an SCV unit will vary depending on the market value of the natural gas, but at a gas cost of $6.00/Mcf would be about $0.09/Mcf, resulting in overall operating costs of $0.17/Mcf for a facility using SCV technology.

EXAMPLE OF REGASIFICATION COSTS	
Total plant capital cost	$1 billion
Plant capacity	1 Bcf/day
Utilization rate	75%
Annual cost of capital	$130 million
Per Mcf cost of capital	$0.461/Mcf
Fuel	$0.09/Mcf
Operating costs	$0.08/Mcf
Total cost of regasification	$0.631/Mcf

Plant capital cost includes interest during construction, and all costs assume SCV technology.

Regasification Infrastructure

Existing Terminals

Today, there are 76 operational receipt terminals worldwide available to receive LNG, with several more in various stages of construction or planning. The majority of existing LNG regasification terminals are located in the Asian market. Japan dominates the receipt arena with 27 terminals located on its shores. Additionally, there are multiple terminals in South Korea, Taiwan, China, and India. There are also multiple terminals in Europe, North America and South America. Total world capacity is approximately 27,000 Bcf/year. A list of worldwide regasification facilities is included in Appendix E.

Future Terminals

As of early 2010, a number of new LNG terminals were under construction. When these terminals are complete they will add significantly to the receiving capacity of the existing major markets. Two new countries – The Netherlands and Thailand – will become importers. When the projects under construction are complete, the world reinjection capacity will have grown by an additional 15%. Numerous additional proposed terminals are in the discussion and planning phases including projects in many countries that do not currently import LNG such as the Bahamas, Croatia, Cyprus, Pakistan, Poland, Singapore, and the UAE. However, with competition between terminals, potential saturation of the market, uncertain financial markets, volatile energy prices, and frequent local opposition, it is hard to know how many proposed projects will actually move forward. Though it seems clear that the actual number moving to construction will be significantly lower than the number currently proposed.

Future Storage Development

While modular onshore tanks offer the latest technology development for more efficient and economic traditional LNG storage, a new type of storage using the Bishop process may dramatically shift the way LNG is regasified, stored and moved to market. The Bishop process uses underground salt domes, either onshore or offshore, as the storage structure. To develop or "build" a salt dome cavern, the salt formation is drilled to the appropriate depth and fresh water is forced down the drill pipe to wash out the storage area. Salt dome storage is relatively inexpensive to develop in comparison to traditional storage tanks. For example, a full containment storage tank capable of holding 3 Bcf of LNG costs over $100 million. But it is estimated that a 3 Bcf salt cavern can be developed for about $15 million. The cost sav-

EXISTING REGASIFICATION FACILITIES BY COUNTRY

Country	Terminals	Capacity (Bcf/yr)
Argentina	1	280
Belgium	1	321
Brazil	2	244
Canada	1	365
Chile	1	122
China	3	575
Dominican Republic	1	88
France	3	906
Greece	1	112
India	2	657
Italy	2	404
Japan	27	9,180
Kuwait	1	146
Mexico	2	550
Portugal	1	195
South Korea	4	3,472
Spain	6	2,157
Taiwan	2	1,018
Turkey	2	448
U.K.	3	838
U.S.	10	5,206

ings allow for development of larger amounts of storage, adding flexibility in delivery to market while also providing the perfect opportunity to blend for Btu content.

Another key difference from traditional storage is the way in which the LNG is regasified. The LNG is off-loaded from the tanker and passed through a heat exchanger in the sea to warm it to 40 degrees Fahrenheit prior to delivery at high pressure (approximately 2,000 psi) into the cavern. The resulting product is then stored in a dense-phase gas form with the high pressure keeping the gas from returning to its traditional gaseous form and volume. In effect, it is simply natural gas under high pressure versus a cryogenic liquid. As the LNG is pulled from storage, the pressure is reduced and the natural gas expands and can then be injected into the pipeline grid. While salt dome storage is in use for other products, no LNG is currently stored in this type of structure. As of early 2010, the Bishop process using salt dome storage is being tested, but is not under currently under development at any project site. Even so, it remains the storage of choice for a few of the offshore terminal proposals.

TERMINALS UNDER CONSTRUCTION		
Country	Terminals	Capacity (Bcf/yr)
Chile	1	73
China	4	536
France	1	292
India	2	390
Italy	2	438
Japan	2	180
Mexico	1	185
Netherlands	1	429
Spain	1	248
Sweden	1	10
Thailand	2	244
U.K.	2	623
U.S.	3	614

As of early 2010. Excludes expansion of existing terminals.

Future Offshore Terminals

We have begun to see use of offshore terminals and some observers believe they may be the wave of the future. With growing opposition to shore-based facilities, offshore facilities allow the siting of LNG away from population centers, but within a cost effective distance. Since offshore facilities may also eliminate the need to dredge deep channels for larger tankers this concept is beginning to gain favor. There are four main types of offshore terminals either currently in use or proposed: gravity-based structures (GBS), conventional fixed platform-based facilities, floating storage and regasification units (FSRU), and regasification vessels.

The GBS terminals are ideal for shallow water (depths of 50 to 75 feet). The GBS structure is designed with concrete or steel structures permanently resting on the sea bottom. The storage tanks are integrated inside the structure with regasification and other essential facilities located on top. The stability of a GBS gives it an advantage over a floating facility with less adverse effects from wind and wave changes when off-loading a tanker. However, GBS terminals can only be located in areas where soil and seismic conditions permit. And, of course, proximity to existing pipeline infrastructure is desirable. As of early 2010, a GBS facility had been completed in Italy and a number of other projects have been proposed elsewhere.

The conventional fixed platform concept has a traditional regasification facility constructed on a platform that is anchored directly into the ocean floor. The platform is similar in design to those commonly used for offshore oil and natural gas wells. A key issue for design of the platform concept is to develop a means of connecting a tanker in moving water that is hundreds of feet below the level of the platform. As of early 2010, no terminals of this type had moved beyond the proposal stage.

The FSRU concept is essentially a tanker with storage and regasification capabilities that is permanently tethered to the sea bottom. LNG deliveries are made by tankers that moor side-by-side with the FSRU facility. The LNG is stored in floating tanks, regasified onboard the floating FSRU facility and then transported via undersea pipeline. The floating facility is intended to be suitable for deep water mooring, but must be designed to contend with additional wave and wind considerations. An advantage to FSRU facilities is that they can be very inexpensive to build and locate. An additional advantage is that FSRU projects can be brought online quickly. But since the facility and the tanker are subject to wind, waves and movement relative to each other, off-loading and delivery to the gas grid become increasingly more challenging. Thus FSRU facilities may require modified tanker designs such as systems that facilitate mooring to a single soft mooring. This allows the vessel to swing freely, subjecting the lowest area possible to wind and wave factors. While this solution has been utilized in the oil industry for decades, it has yet to be implemented for LNG facilities. As of early 2010, two FSRU terminals were operational with an additional terminal under construction in Italy.

A similar concept to FSRU is an offshore terminal designed to accept gas from regasification vessels that are not permanently moored but are free to travel at will. The vessels are similar to traditional LNG tankers, but included on the ship deck is a complete regasification facility. In addition to the regasification vessel, the system consists of either an offshore submerged off-loading buoy that is connected to an undersea pipeline or a dockside receiving system that allows the regasification vessel to dock and inject gas into a dockside onshore pipeline. Like the FSRU technology, receiving terminals are inexpensive to build and can be brought online quickly. The regasification vessel concept also has the advantage of flexibility in that it bypasses the need to build permanent terminals committed to a specific market and allows cargo owners to choose the most profitable markets on an ongoing basis. As of early 2010, three offshore regasification terminal projects were operational, two using off-shore buoys in the U.S., one using dockside facilities in the U.K, with an additional U.S. project under construction.

With the exception of the FSRU and regasification vessel concept, offshore terminals are forecast to cost as much or more than their onshore counterparts. While the marine facilities are significantly less expensive (just $25 to $40 million) since breakwaters, jetties and trestles are not needed, the platform, storage tanks, regasification facilities, and support structures are more costly than for onshore facilities. Total costs of GBS or fixed platform facilities have been estimated at $600 to $1 billion for a 1 Bcf facility, which is similar to current onshore costs. However, if additional projects go to construction they may find that actual costs exceed earlier estimates.

Key Issues

As the worldwide market for LNG continues to grow, there are several key regasification issues to watch. Site approval is becoming more contentious throughout North America and parts of Europe. In the U.S., the Energy Policy Act of 2005 has given the FERC final authority over terminal siting. Without the right of federal eminent domain, however, land cannot be condemned for siting purposes. Even with site approval, there are still state, local and special interest group roadblocks to overcome. All of these issues may result in significant delays in gaining necessary approvals as well as additional expenses in construction.

LNG interchangeability, or the lack of a standardized LNG product continues to be a growing problem for U.S. and European markets. With Japan as the largest purchaser of LNG, it is not surprising that most liquefaction was built to suit its higher Btu content needs. As the North American market grows in market share, more attention will be paid to its market specifications. This will serve to lower the Btu content of LNG being shipped in the Atlantic Basin. However, with a growing spot market and rising trend in physical swapping, the market must be prepared on both the production and the receiving end to manage the variable Btu content.

In the U.S. and Europe, where LNG is a small portion of total supply, the downstream pipelines and distribution systems are currently capable of absorbing the spikes in gas volume received from LNG vaporization. As more and more terminals are connected to the pipeline grid and LNG becomes a larger part of the gas supply picture, pipeline and storage capacity between terminals and markets will need to be expanded to accommodate the movement of incremental supply. It is possible that one area will become oversupplied and will have inadequate capacity to move the gas to the most needy markets. Thus the pipeline grid and storage capabilities will be major factors in determining the success of LNG as an ongoing supply source. Other countries such as India and China, which are newly developing their LNG industries, will also require significant investments in downstream storage and pipeline facilities.

Another key issue to watch is the actual implementation of new technology in offshore terminals and storage. While concepts such as GBS and fixed platform-based terminals are not new to the energy industry, their adaptation and use with LNG have yet to be tested in long-term operation. Concepts such as the Bishop process for salt dome storage have the potential to radically change the cost structure for regasification terminals. New innovations in subsea cryogenic pipelines using next generation insulation such as Izoflex can reduce the marine costs by up to 40% by removing the need for a trestle. Unlike traditional foam insulation used in cryogenic pipe, products such as Izoflex do not require replacement every ten years, reducing operating expenses over the life of the facility as well. FSRU and regasification vessel systems that require no permanent regasification terminal have potential spot market implications worldwide. All of these technology changes bear watching as they could move the market in a variety of directions.

Lastly, safety and security will continue to be critical issues. Since worst case accident or attack scenarios can result in catastrophic results, the siting and design of regasification facilities will continue to be a contentious issue in many areas. And one major accident or terrorist attack could completely alter the landscape.

What you will learn:

- The key safety and security issues relating to LNG

- The history of LNG safety and security

- What the industry is doing to address safety and security issues

- The key environmental issues relating to LNG

- How the industry is addressing environmental issues

- How LNG risks compare to other industries

SECTION SIX: SAFETY AND ENVIRONMENTAL CONCERNS

There are currently 26 LNG liquefaction facilities, 76 LNG terminals, over 330 LNG tankers, and over 200 LNG storage facilities throughout the world. As many countries move forward with expansion of LNG capabilities and communities consider siting of new LNG facilities, questions about LNG's safety and environmental impacts have taken center stage. From a safety standpoint, there are a number of concerns: the danger of injury or property damage due to spilling of extremely cold liquids, the normal dangers associated with natural gas once LNG has been regasified, the potential for catastrophic pool fires or vapor cloud fires, and the all-important question of whether terrorists could exploit such possibilities. From an environmental standpoint, potential impacts include air emissions, cold water discharge and land-use issues. In this Section we will take a closer look at the various safety and environmental impacts of LNG.

Safety Issues

The key safety issues for LNG relate to the consequences of an LNG spill[1]. Most significant is the potential for ignition of an LNG pool or vapor cloud. Models indicate that under the right conditions, a fire igniting an LNG pool or vapor cloud could cause extensive damage to life and property. Other less significant issues include the potential for freeze burns, cracking of metals, explosions due to leaking natural gas, and flameless explosion. We will address these safety issues later in this Section. But first, a look at the physical properties of LNG.

---

[1] The information in this Section is based on reports prepared by the Congressional Research Service (*Liquefied Natural Gas (LNG) Infrastructure Security: Issues for Congress*, March 16, 2005 and *Liquefied Natural Gas (LNG) Import Terminals: Siting, Safety and Regulation*, April 20, 2005), various presentations by Jerry Havens and Tom Spicer of the Chemical Hazards Research Center at the University of Arkansas, the California Energy Commission Staff Consultant Report titled *International and National Efforts to Address the Safety and Security Risks of Importing Liquefied Natural Gas: A Compendium*, January 2005, the Sandia Report, SAND2004-6258, *Guidance on Risk Analysis and Safety Implications of a Large Liquefied Natural Gas (LNG) Spill Over Water*, GAO-07-316 *Maritime Security: Public Safety Consequences of a Terrorist Attack on a Tanker Carrying Liquefied Natural Gas Need Clarification*, and SAND2008-3153 *Breach and Safety Analysis of Spills over Water from Large Liquefied Natural Gas Carriers*.

SECTION SIX: SAFETY AND ENVIRONMENTAL CONCERNS

Physical Properties of LNG

To fully understand the potential safety and environmental impacts of LNG, you must first understand its physical properties. As we have discussed, LNG is simply natural gas that is cooled below –260 degrees Fahrenheit. When allowed to warm above this temperature, LNG will revert to its natural gaseous state with properties no different from natural gas that has never been liquefied. Natural gas is lighter than air, so when released it will rise and disperse unless it is confined within a physical enclosed space. LNG is heavier than air but lighter than water, and if spilled on water it will float until it warms and returns to its gaseous state. Small amounts of LNG vaporize very rapidly when they come in contact with warmer air or water, which is why we use the term "boil-off" to describe LNG becoming gaseous. LNG spills are not toxic and leave no residue once the gas has dispersed.

LNG is not combustible in liquid state, but when gaseous can ignite when concentration of the gas (i.e., gas/air ratio) is between 5% and 15%. If the gas is in a confined space at this gas/air ratio and is ignited, an explosion can occur. If not confined, the gas will simply burn until there is no longer sufficient fuel and/or air to maintain the 5% to 15% concentration.

Specific Safety Concerns

Much of the concern for LNG accidents is focused on the potential for a rapid spill of large volumes. In such cases, the physical properties of LNG may prevent harmless vaporization and dissipation into the atmosphere. Here's why. Following a large spill, the LNG would pool on the ground or water until it warmed to the point where it became gas. As the top surface warmed, the pool would begin to give off LNG vapor. The LNG vapor would be heavy because it is cool. Mixtures of dry air and cold methane vapor are heavier than air, and in the absence of either heat from the ground or water or humidity in the air, the vapor remains heavier than air. This would cause it to float just above the ground or water. Thus, if the LNG vapor remained heavier than the surrounding air, a vapor cloud similar to ground fog would tend to form. This vapor cloud would spread slowly in the absence of wind, or more rapidly if wind is present.

The possible ignition of an LNG pool or vapor cloud is considered the primary hazard associated with the LNG industry. Opinions as to how great an area would be affected by a pool or vapor fire are mixed based on assumptions used. The 2004 study by Sandia Laboratories concluded that for a very large accidental spill near shore, the most significant impacts[2] would occur within a distance of 300 meters (984 feet) with lesser impacts at a distance of 750 meters (2,460 feet). The same study concluded that for a very large intentional spill over water (e.g., a terrorist attack) the affected distances are 500 meters (1,640 feet) for most significant impacts and 1,600 meters (5,249 feet, or nearly one mile) for lesser impacts. In the 2008 study of the largest newbuild vessels, the estimated spill rates and spill volumes increased slightly, some 7-8%. However, even with the modest increase, the most significant impacts to public safety and property near shore are still within the distances identified in the 2004 study.

There are a number of specific hazards that could result from an LNG spill, as well as a few other areas of concern. Each is discussed below.

Pool Fires

If LNG is spilled near an ignition source, the potential exists for the vaporizing gas to immediately ignite and burn above the LNG pool. If the LNG pool were not confined, it could spread quickly – especially on water. This could result in a pool fire expanding over a large area. This fire would burn at a much higher temperature than oil or gasoline fires and could not be extinguished. It would simply continue to burn until all the fuel had been consumed. The thermal radiation from such a fire could injure or kill people and damage property at a distance far from the actual fire itself.

Vapor Cloud Fires

There is also a second type of fire possible. If LNG spills but does not immediately ignite, then a vapor cloud may form. This vapor cloud would drift from the spill site according to wind conditions. If the vapor cloud were to come in contact with an

---

[2]"Significant impacts" are generally understood to include major injuries to people and major structural damage to critical infrastructure.

ignition source while the gas/air ratio is between 5% to 15%, then the cloud would catch fire. The fire would likely be smaller and less intense than a pool fire because only a portion of the fuel within the cloud would be at a combustible gas/air mix. However, the fire could burn its way back to the LNG spill where the cloud originated, in which case the fire could act as an ignition source for the remaining LNG pool, resulting in the vapor cloud fire becoming a pool fire. Because vapor cloud fires are smaller than pool fires, the distance at which thermal radiation effects would be a concern is much smaller. But because vapor cloud fires could move rapidly in heavy winds, the distance from the fire at risk for a hazardous situation is much greater. As with a pool fire, a moving vapor cloud fire would continue to burn until the combustible fuel-air mix no longer existed.

Rapid Phase Transition Explosion

A third theoretical danger is known as a rapid phase transition explosion or "flameless explosion" resulting from LNG heating up very quickly and converting to gaseous state so rapidly that pressure changes result in a shock wave. Studies to date indicate that such an explosion is highly unlikely, and that if it were to occur it would affect a much smaller area than either pool or vapor cloud fires. A rapid phase transition explosion could cause some injury to individuals directly in the area and/or localized structural damage, although impacts would likely be minor.

Additional Hazards of Leaking or Spilled LNG

Other hazards of spilled LNG include the potential for asphyxiation, freeze burns and cracking of metals. While LNG is not poisonous, an individual trapped in the center of a vapor cloud could asphyxiate due to lack of oxygen. Because of its temperature, contact with skin can result in severe freeze burns. And contact with certain metals, will cause them to crack. LNG that leaks and becomes regasified and then migrates to an enclosure can result in explosion if the gas/air concentration is at the right level and a source of ignition is present. However, this danger is no more significant than the danger of explosion from any natural gas source.

While all of these hazard types are feasible results of an accidental or intentional release of LNG, to date no actual incidents have occurred. Even the expert studies that continue to look at the dangers are forced to use theoretical data and sophisticated models due to lack of actual experience.

LNG and Terrorism

In a world where terrorism dominates the daily headlines, it's not surprising that there is a growing fear that LNG tankers, onshore processing facilities and storage tanks could provide a ready target for terrorists. Especially given that LNG infrastructure is highly visible and easily identified. Concerns include physical attacks resulting in fires, hijacking of tankers for use as weapons and attacks designed to result in supply interruptions. The risks of such attacks include damage to individuals and property near onshore facilities, damage to individuals and property near shipping paths, damage to ships near a tanker, damage to the tanker itself, and the economic effects stemming from an interruption of natural gas supply.

LNG tankers are perhaps most vulnerable because they are more difficult to secure and because LNG spills on water are more difficult to control than those occurring on land. Studies have suggested that a small-scale missile or bomb attack could breach an LNG tanker resulting in an LNG spill and, assuming a source of ignition, a significant fire. Many preventative safety systems have been developed to lessen the possibility of tanker attack within the zone that could impact the public and property. After the terrorist attacks of 9/11, the U.S. Congress enacted the Maritime Transportation Security Act, giving the U.S. Coast Guard lead responsibility for maritime security. Before an LNG carrier is allowed within U.S. territorial waters (19 kilometers or 12 miles of the coast), Coast Guard teams board and thoroughly search the vessel, checking identification and performing safety and system inspections. Once all the safety and security procedures have been completed, the vessel is allowed into U.S. territorial waters. Like aircraft, a moving safety zone is established around the vessel as it proceeds into port, keeping a safe distance between the carrier and other vessels. While the safety rules do not eliminate the threat of terrorism, they do act as a deterrent.

Similarly, attacks could result in spills from onshore storage tanks and/or processing facilities. Onshore spills, however, are easier to contain and onshore facilities are perhaps easier to protect than a moving tanker. Just as with tankers, onshore facilities are designed with safety in mind. Every storage tank is secured within a physical berm sized to contain more than 100% of the LNG tank volume, assuring full containment

SECTION SIX: SAFETY AND ENVIRONMENTAL CONCERNS

if the tank ruptures by accident or an act of terrorism. Liquids from ruptured pipes would flow and accumulate in one of several catch basins designed throughout the facility where they would evaporate. Emergency shutdown systems are also in place. Besides the physical safety systems, security and monitoring systems are also in place restricting entrance to the facilities and sensitive areas.

Risks Relative to Other Industries

Just about everyone, including the staunchest of LNG proponents, will admit to the possibility that LNG could cause great damage given "perfect storm" conditions. Yet any potential threats are perhaps more fairly viewed when compared with threats from other substances that are faced on a daily basis. For communities near onshore facilities or tanker routes, the risks are probably similar to those associated with oil refineries and chemical processing facilities. The risk of destruction of a tanker and nearby ships is probably higher than oil tankers (since oil is not explosive) but less than liquefied petroleum (LPG) and gasoline tankers, both of which are common in U.S. waters[3]. Disruption of supply by attacks on ships and/or terminal facilities would probably have a minimal impact on overall natural gas supply in any given area since the amount of gas delivered by a specific LNG facility or tanker is typically small relative to the area's overall supply picture. This risk may be higher in countries where LNG accounts for a higher proportion of the natural gas supply mix.

When comparing risks between the LNG industry and other industries, we must also consider that the number of LNG shipments and facilities is significantly smaller than that of other hazardous industries. A recent report to Congress stated that over 500 toxic chemical facilities operate in urban areas of the U.S. where worst case accidents could affect 100,000 or more people – including chlorine plants in city water systems and ammonia tanks used in agricultural fertilizer production. There are also numerous oil refineries and LPG terminals operating in U.S. ports and over 100,000 annual U.S. shipments of hazardous marine cargo such as ammonia, crude oil, LPG, and other volatile chemicals[4]. LNG shipments would make up less than 1% of the United States' total hazardous material shipments. While other areas of the world certainly have varying circumstances, for most countries the risks from LNG are similarly minimal when compared with other potentially hazardous industries.

---

[3]Waryas, E., Lloyd's Register America's, Inc., "Major Disaster Planning: Understanding and Managing Your Risk." Presentation to the Fourth National Harbor Safety Committee Conference, Galveston, TX, 2002.

[4]CRS Report for Congress, *Liquefied Natural Gas (LNG) Import Terminals: Siting, Safety and Regulation.*

The Historical Safety Record of LNG

Given the 70-year history of use of LNG for storage, and the 45-year history of its transport by tankers, the number of LNG accidents has been surprisingly small. And as of early 2010, there were no known terrorist attacks on LNG facilities or tankers. Following is a brief summary of each of the accidents to date:

- Cleveland, Ohio, 1944: An LNG storage tank failed resulting in a vapor cloud that filled surrounding streets and the storm sewer system. The vapor cloud ignited resulting in 128 deaths. The tank failure was due to substandard tank construction, the result of a shortage of stainless steel alloy during World War II. The steel alloy that was used had low nickel content resulting in a brittle tank that failed when exposed to cold LNG. Tanks built to current standards have never had a similar failure. This facility did not have an impoundment dike to contain the spilled LNG within the facility grounds (which would have diminished the size of the vapor cloud).

- Staten Island, New York, 1973: An LNG peak-shaving plant was taken out of service and emptied of LNG so that repairs could be made. During the repair work, vapor associated with a cleaning process ignited the tank liner. The resulting fire raised the temperature in the tank resulting in a pressure increase that dislodged the concrete roof. The roof fell on the workers in the tank killing 37 people. The New York fire department concluded that the accident was construction-related since LNG was not in any way responsible for the accident.

- Cove Point, Maryland, 1979: An explosion occurred within an electrical substation at the Cove Point LNG terminal. The explosion occurred because LNG had leaked through an inadequately tightened LNG pump seal, vaporized into natural gas, traveled through 200 feet of underground electrical conduit, and entered the substation. The natural gas/air mixture was ignited by sparks from a circuit breaker resulting in an explosion. The explosion killed one operator and caused about $3 million in damages.

- Skikda, Algeria, 2004: A portion of an LNG liquefaction facility was destroyed following the explosion of a gas vapor cloud within the facility, killing 27 workers and injuring 56 more. The explosion and the resulting fire destroyed three LNG trains, but the fire was contained before spreading further. Three adjacent LNG trains and the LNG storage tanks at the facility were not damaged. A definitive cause for the fire has yet to be made public, although reports indicate that a vapor cloud of gas formed in the facility due to a leak and was ignited. It appears that maintenance issues associated with the facility may have contributed to the accident.

SECTION SIX: SAFETY AND ENVIRONMENTAL CONCERNS

- Marine Spills: In over 45 years, there have been more than 80,000 voyages worldwide by LNG tankers. Throughout this period there have been eight marine spills and seven marine incidents without spills. None of these resulted in cargo fires, explosions or fatalities.

Handling Safety and Security Issues

Preventing spills and containing damage when they occur are key factors in the design, construction and operation of LNG tankers and facilities. And because of the potential for catastrophic damage, security procedures are an integral part of their operational procedures. The following standards apply specifically to the U.S. While security procedures will vary from country to country, similar standards apply to most other worldwide facilities.

As you learned in Section Four, LNG tankers must follow international design and safety procedure standards, and if they are active in U.S. waters, even more stringent U.S. standards. These standards are designed to prevent leaks, groundings, collisions, and steering or propulsion failures and to identify any problems that may occur promptly. LNG tankers are constructed with cargo tanks that are housed inside a double-walled hull using materials that are resistant to puncture. Unlike single-hulled oil tankers, which may leak if the single hull is breached, LNG tankers will not leak unless both hulls and a cargo tank are breached. To prevent grounding or collisions, ship handling safety features include radar and global positioning systems that alert the crew to other traffic and hazards around the ship, distress signaling systems and beacons that automatically notify authorities if a ship is in difficulty, and systems that continuously monitor the performance of the ship's steering and propulsion systems. While in transit within ports, safety procedures include traffic control, safety zones around the tanker, escort by Coast Guard vessels, and coordination with local law enforcement and public safety agencies. The cargo is continuously monitored so that any abnormal situations are noted rapidly and mitigation procedures implemented immediately. Ships are all equipped with gas and fire detection systems so that any leaks or fires are detected almost instantly. Additional security measures recently implemented in the U.S. include a requirement of four days' notice prior to a ship's planned arrival, investigation of crew backgrounds and random security inspections. In the U.S., LNG vessels are boarded by marine safety personnel prior to port entry to verify that all safety systems are working properly. Similar procedures are used in other countries. Unlike for onshore facilities, exclusion zones around tankers are not considered practical since no entity has the authority to control space around a tanker at sea. However, some ports do restrict other ship traffic when an LNG tanker is entering or leaving.

Design and safety procedure standards for onshore and future offshore terminals are determined by the country in which the facility is located (or within whose waters the offshore terminals are located). As discussed in Section Five, terminal facilities include the docking facility, LNG storage tanks, the regasification equipment, and gas handling infrastructure. Safety procedures must encompass all activities at the terminal. The system that transfers LNG from the ship to the storage tank has shutdown equipment that automatically stops pumps, closes valves and removes the transfer arm during emergencies. As an additional precaution on most vessels, a water curtain is constantly flowing on the side of the tanker during cargo unloading to protect it in the event of any cargo spillage from the loading arms. Deluge systems on the ship can also be deployed to protect the vessel in case of a spill or the ignition of gas vapors. All tanks are designed with double walls and modern design full containment tanks have the additional protection of an outer concrete tank and a steel reinforced concrete roof. Tanks and regasification facilities are continuously monitored and are equipped to automatically release unsafe pressures and shut down during non-standard conditions. These facilities also have gas and fire detection systems as well as fire response systems.

Onshore LNG facilities are situated within a basin and surrounded by berms called impoundment dikes that are designed to contain a volume of LNG greater than the maximum possible spill. If a spill were to occur, the dikes would keep the LNG pool from moving beyond the facility grounds. All onshore facilities are also required to maintain an exclusion zone. An exclusion zone is an area around the facility in which the owner has legal control over all activities and where only LNG processing is allowed. There are two types of exclusion zones – thermal radiation zones which provide protection for the heat of fires at the facility, and vapor dispersion zones which provide protection from migrating and potentially flammable vapor clouds. Modeling is used to determine safe distances from both hazards and the necessary size of the exclusion zones. An exclusion zone is unique to each facility. For example, the exclusion zones for the Cove Point LNG facility cover 1,107 acres while the exclusion zones for the Elba Island facility cover 840 acres.

Finally, facility design must also consider the potential impacts of earthquakes. Studies of geologic conditions and earthquake history at a proposed LNG site are required to determine appropriate design loads on the critical components of the LNG plant.

SECTION SIX: SAFETY AND ENVIRONMENTAL CONCERNS

These components must then be designed and constructed for LNG containment during and after a 1 in 10,000-year earthquake. This design was put to the test in 2007 when a 6.8 earthquake hit Japan. While the earthquake resulted in enough damage to shut down a nuclear facility for 21 months, no damage to any of the LNG storage tanks at the numerous terminals throughout the island was reported. Owners of LNG terminals are also required to designate security officers, perform security assessments, develop and implement security procedures, and develop and maintain emergency response plans.

Environmental Issues

As with any commercial process, LNG facilities are responsible for a number or environmental impacts that include air emissions, cold water discharge, land use, and possible discharge of LNG during an accident. And as with safety concerns, environmental impacts are best viewed in comparison to other industries. Air emissions are considered to be minimal. Leaks of natural gas into the atmosphere are very small and the most significant source of air emissions is associated with either the diesel engines used by tug boats escorting tankers or the diesel generators used by ships while in port. If spilled on water or land, LNG will not mix with the water or soil, but rather evaporates and dissipates into the air leaving no residue. LNG terminals do not consume large amounts of water or emit waste into water. However, terminals using ORV technology present environmental concerns since they may use seawater for the warming necessary for regasification. This process cools the water in the terminal's vicinity, potentially impacting the local ecosystem. Dredging and filling activities associated with constructing and maintaining harbors for large tankers may also have impacts on marine water quality and marine life. Although there is no ballast water discharge by tankers in countries receiving LNG shipments, the tankers do take on ballast water for the return journey that is discharged at the LNG supply port. This practice could introduce non-native species into the marine environment in those countries. Construction of terminals in pristine areas may also have impacts on land ecosystems. And noise, visual and traffic impacts may occur at specific locations. In the event of a spill, environmental damage would be confined to fire and freezing impacts near the spill since LNG dissipates completely as it warms and leaves no residue.

Conclusions

While the safety, security and environmental impacts of LNG tankers and facilities have rightfully been given serious scrutiny, the potential risks are relatively small when compared to other industries whose activities place hundreds of thousands in harms way on a daily basis. Although levels of risk vary depending on models and assumptions used, most in-depth studies have concluded that the risks from accidental spills are relatively small and manageable with current safety procedures. The risks from intentional events such as terrorism, although larger, can be mitigated through safety and security measures. Environmental impacts are generally considered to be negligible relative to the benefits of increased usage of the environmentally favorable natural gas fuel. Lastly, it should be noted that depending on the circumstances surrounding an incident, there is potential for significant monetary liability on the part of LNG tanker and facility owners. This provides solid motivation for them to take safety and security seriously.

What you will learn:

- Why the LNG business is regulated
- Who regulates what
- How liquefaction facilities are regulated
- How shipping is regulated
- How regasification terminals and downstream pipelines are regulated
- Details on permitting for new LNG regasification terminals

SECTION SEVEN: REGULATION AND PERMITTING

Regulation

Most aspects of the LNG business are highly regulated due to safety and security concerns at all points along the delivery chain. Regasification facilities are also commonly regulated from the standpoint of being part of the monopoly utility/pipeline infrastructure within a specific country. Given the global nature of the business, regulation of multiple jurisdictions applies throughout the delivery chain. In general, regulations and permitting procedures serve a variety of purposes:

- Ensuring that environmental impacts are acceptable and mitigated where possible.
- Ensuring facilities are operated in a safe manner.
- Ensuring security against deliberate attacks.
- Providing for fair pricing and a reasonable rate-of-return for monopoly facilities.
- Providing for fair third-party access to monopoly facilities.
- Ensuring that the design and construction of new facilities is subject to all applicable laws and regulations.
- In some cases, determining a need for new facilities before construction is authorized.
- In some cases, approving export of natural gas resources and terms of gas supply agreements.
- Ensuring that operation of LNG facilities does not negatively impact downstream pipelines and customers.

These concerns may not apply to all parts of the LNG delivery chain equally, and are addressed differently in different countries. In this Section, we will consider regulation of each of the three key parts of the delivery chain: liquefaction, shipping and regasification. Since offshore facilities are sometimes regulated differently, we will consider those facilities separately.

SECTION SEVEN: REGULATION AND PERMITTING

REGULATION OF THE LNG INDUSTRY		
What is Regulated?	**How is It Regulated?**	**Why is It Regulated?**
LIQUEFACTION		
Need for new facilities	Usually federal regulator or government agency; may be deregulated in some countries	To ensure consistency with overall resource development plans and to foster highest value resource development
Technical design of facilities	Usually federal regulator and one or more federal and local agencies	To ensure design is in compliance with all laws concerning safety, security and environmental protection
Supply and liquefaction agreements – price and terms	Usually federal regulator or government agency; may be deregulated in some countries	To ensure export gas is not needed for local consumption; protection of local revenue streams
Operations – safety, security and environmental compliance	Usually standards set by federal agencies	To ensure operation is in compliance with all laws concerning safety, security and environmental protection
SHIPPING		
Technical design of ships	International Maritime Organization (IMO) rules plus federal regulations for operations within a specific country's waters	To ensure tankers are built to safe standards
Operations – safety, security and environmental compliance	IMO rules plus federal regulations for operations within a specific country's waters	To ensure that tankers are operated in a safe and secure manner without unacceptable impacts on the environment
REGASIFICATION		
Need for new facilities	Usually federal regulator or government agency; may be deregulated in some countries	To ensure consistency with overall resource development plans and to foster least-cost supply
Technical design of facilities	Usually federal regulator and one or more federal and/or local agencies	To ensure design is in compliance with all laws concerning safety, security and environmental protection
Third-party access	Federal regulator, may be deregulated in some countries	To ensure fair access to market participants given the monopoly function
Price and terms of service	Federal regulator, may be deregulated in some countries	To encourage construction of needed facilities, ensure fair pricing and terms of service, establish a reasonable rate of return, and to prevent negative impacts on downstream pipelines or customers
Operations – safety, security and environmental compliance	Usually standards set by federal agencies	To ensure operation is in compliance with all laws concerning safety, security and environmental protection

Liquefaction Facilities

To date, most liquefaction facilities have been built as part of a dedicated project associated with a long-term gas supply agreement that covers a significant portion of the plant's output. As you have learned, these facilities are enormously expensive, and would not likely be built without long-term commitments in place. The new exception to this rule is floating LNG liquefaction. Since the liquefaction facility is mounted on an LNG vessel, its very design allows the movement from one small-to-medium stranded gas field to another as an economic option to recover proved reserves. Because the facility fits on a ship-sized deck, the total capital involved is also significantly less than the mega trains being built today. However, the same regulatory concepts still apply. Both the need for the project and the specifics of the gas supply agreement are usually reviewed by one or more federal government agencies and/or regulators in the producing country. Review typically includes an assessment of the complete national resource base and the nation's own natural gas needs. This is to assure that the gas sold through the facility is not needed locally for at least a number of years into the future. This also ensures that exportation of this gas is consistent with government plans for maximizing the value of national resources. Since gas resources are often owned or highly regulated by federal governments, and liquefaction facilities are often (at least) partially government-owned, the price and terms associated with gas supply and liquefaction agreements are often subject to review and/or direct negotiation with the federal government. Technical design for new facilities is also reviewed by federal and, in some cases, local agencies to ensure safe design and compliance with environmental laws. And once facilities are operational, operating procedures are usually reviewed by federal and/or local agencies to ensure safety, security and environmental compliance.

In the U.S., there is only one liquefaction facility – the Kenai LNG Export Terminal in the Cook Inlet Basin area of Alaska. On April 19, 1967, the Kenai terminal was granted authorization to export LNG under Section 3 of the Natural Gas Act (NGA). The Order also addressed a request for a Presidential Permit for the construction, operation and maintenance of the Kenai LNG terminal. Since a Presidential Permit applies only to a facility located on a border which physically connects two countries, the request was dismissed as unnecessary. However, the original Order did not address the siting, construction, operation, and maintenance of the Kenai LNG terminal. In later years, FERC's jurisdiction under Section 3 of NGA was clarified to include authority over the siting, construction, operation, and maintenance of LNG terminals, generally geared toward regasification facilities. In the Energy Policy Act of 2005, a new provision was added to the NGA, clarifying that FERC has "the exclusive authority" for such approvals whether they are liquefaction or regasification. Today, the Kenai liquefaction terminal must comply with the same Section 3 reporting and inspection requirements applicable to all other operational regasification terminals in the United States. In particular, FERC ordered a cryogenic design and technical review of the Kenai LNG terminal, with staff authorized to make recommendations for facility modifications. The terminal is now subject to regular technical reviews and site inspections. Additionally, FERC ordered that semi-annual operational reports and significant incident reports for the terminal be filed.

Regulation of this facility is shared with two other agencies. The U.S. Coast Guard oversees safety and security in the marine transfer area of LNG terminals, which includes facilities between where the ship moors and the first shut-off valve on the pipeline (immediately before the receiving storage tanks). Safety issues monitored by the Coast Guard include facility design, gas detection systems and alarms, firefighting equipment, and approval of the terminal's operations and emergency manuals and training programs. The remainder of the facility is regulated by the Department of Transportation's (DOT) Pipeline and Hazardous Materials Safety Agency which enforces similar safety regulations. The DOT's rules incorporate standards from the National Fire Protection Agency (NFPA) covering many procedures for preventing and responding to accidents. Following 9/11, new security rules were mandated by the Maritime Transportation Security Act of 2002, requiring LNG terminal operators to conduct facility security assessments and implement security plans. The security plan includes provisions to keep the facilities secure such as access control measures, security measures for cargo handling and deliveries, surveillance and monitoring plans, communication plans, incident procedures, and training and drill requirements. Unlike safety responsibilities, which are split between the Coast Guard and the DOT, security regulations are overseen solely by the Coast Guard throughout the entire facility. The Energy Policy Act of 2005 generally removed safety, security and environmental authority from state agencies' direct jurisdiction, although state agencies may continue to monitor such issues and report concerns to the applicable federal agency.

Shipping

All LNG ships in international service are required to comply with rules specified in international treaties. The organization that administers these rules is the International Maritime Organization (IMO) which is a United Nations agency responsible for improving the safety and security of international shipping and preventing marine pollution from ships[1]. All LNG ships must also comply with specific design, construction and operation codes to ensure safe operation and the ship's ability to withstand collisions, running aground, onboard accidents, and loss of steering and/or propulsion systems. Tougher security standards have recently been added to those developed at the SOLAS Convention (see footnote) and are covered in the International Ship and Port Facility Security Code (ISPS Code). These include detailed mandatory security requirements for governments, port authorities and shipping companies as well as recommended guidelines for meeting them.

For LNG ships operating in U.S. waters, even more stringent safety and security standards are appended to the international standards. These include requirements for enhanced grades of steel designed to arrest cracks in hulls, design for higher stresses in certain types of LNG tanks, and prohibiting the use of venting as a means of cargo temperature or pressure control. Before operating in U.S. waters, owners of LNG tankers must submit vessel plans and other information to the Coast Guard for review. Ships passing this review are granted a Certificate of Compliance which is valid for two years, but subject to annual review. LNG tankers are often boarded by Coast Guard personnel upon entering U.S. territorial waters to verify that key navigation, safety, fire fighting, and cargo control systems are operating properly. Additional U.S. security standards include 96 hours advance notice of ship arrivals with information on last ports of call and crew identities, at-sea boarding where Coast Guard personnel conduct security sweeps, traffic control when an LNG ship is entering or exiting port, safety zones around ships to prevent other vessels from approaching, and escorts by Coast Guard patrol craft when in and near port.

Regasification Facilities

Regasification facilities are subject to regulations on safety, security and environmental protection. Regasification facilities are also often subject to ratemaking and terms of service regulation although many countries, including the U.S., are choosing to reduce some regulation to encourage new facilities to be built. As with liquefaction terminals, technical design for new facilities is reviewed by federal and, in some cases, local agencies to ensure safe design, and compliance with environmental laws and security standards. Once facilities are operational, operating procedures are usually reviewed by federal and/or local agencies to ensure safety, security and environmental

---

[1] Applicable IMO rules include regulations set at the International Convention for the Safety of Life at Sea ("SOLAS Convention") and the International Convention for the Prevention of Pollution from Ships ("MARPOL Convention"), and the International Code for the Construction and Equipment of Ships Carrying Liquefied Gases in Bulk ("IGC Code").

SECTION SEVEN: REGULATION AND PERMITTING

compliance. In the U.S. these reviews, as outlined in the Energy Policy Act of 2005, are exclusively under federal jurisdiction with an advisory role assigned to the states.

Ratemaking and terms of service regulation are generally handled by a federal regulatory agency. Key issues include whether open access[2] to third parties is required, how services are to be priced and how strictly to regulate contractual terms or terms of service. In Asia, gas markets are generally not deregulated to the point that open access has become an issue. In Europe, LNG facilities are subject to European Union directives that require TPA (third-party access) arrangements with the exception that regulators within a country can exempt LNG facilities if they can demonstrate that:

> **KEY U.S. LAWS AND REGULATIONS COVERING LNG FACILITIES**
>
> - Energy Policy Act of 2005
> - Title 49 Code of Federal Regulations (CFR) Part 193 – Liquefied Natural Gas Facilities: Federal Safety Standards
> - Title 33 CFR Part 127 – Waterfront Facilities Handling Liquefied Natural Gas and Liquefied Hazardous Gas (LHG)
> - National Fire Protection Agency (NFPA) 59A – Standards for the Production, Storage, and Handling of LNG
> - Deepwater Port Acts of 1974 and 2002
> - National Environmental Policy Act
> - Title 33 CFR Part 106 – Maritime Security: Outer Continental Shelf Facilities
> - Clean Water Act
> - Clean Air Act
> - Coastal Zone Management Act

- Investments enhance competition in or security of gas supply.
- An exemption is needed to allow investment to occur.
- Fair charges are levied on all users of the facility.
- The exemption is not detrimental to competition and/or the functioning of internal gas markets or pipeline systems.

These exceptions are generally granted on a "use it or lose it" basis. The terminal owner is granted exclusive use of terminal capacity. However, if the exclusive capacity is not utilized, regulators reserve the right to revisit the terms and/or grant third party open access. Such a recall actually occurred in the U.K in 2008.

---

[2] Open access refers to a requirement that owners of LNG facilities must act as a public utility in making the facility available to any interested party under non-discriminatory terms and conditions. In Europe this is known as TPA, or third-party access.

In much of North America, the regulatory bodies generally recognize the value of open access but since the Hackberry Decision in 2002 have allowed new project sponsors to reserve capacity at their discretion, believing that open access rules will impede development of new facilities. Pricing methodologies include traditional cost-of-service regulation with rates tied to costs plus an authorized rate-of-return for pre-Hackberry facilities and market-based pricing where project owners are allowed to negotiate pricing with parties wishing to use their facilities. Many countries in Europe use cost-of-service pricing, while other European countries and most of the rest of the world use market-based pricing. The same is true relative to other terms of service. Some European countries mandate tariffed terms of service while elsewhere negotiated terms of service are the norm (in some cases, with review to ensure operators are not exploiting a monopoly position unfairly).

In the U.S., safety, security and environmental protection for regasification terminals are covered by the same laws and agencies that cover liquefaction facilities (see page 80). Ratemaking and terms of service regulation are subject to Federal Energy Regulatory Commission (FERC) jurisdiction. Current FERC policy, as laid out in the Energy Policy Act of 2005, holds that for new facilities and expansions:

REGULATION OF NEW REGASIFICATION FACILITY SERVICES

European Union Regulatory Policy (unless an exemption is granted by the regulator within the country where the facility is located):

- Facility owners are required not to discriminate between parties or classes of parties.

- Facility owners can refuse access only on the basis of lack of capacity due to public service obligations, or where such access would result in serious economic or financial difficulties to the operator as a result of take-or-pay contracts.

- Any negotiated access terms must conclude in voluntary commercial agreements.

- Any regulated access terms must conform to published tariffs and/or terms of service.

U.S. Regulatory Policy (for new projects approved after 2002):

- Facility owners are not required to provide for open access.

- Facility owners are not subject to regulation of rates, charges or terms of service.

- Facility owners are not required to file contracts with a regulator.

- Rates and terms of service may be negotiated.
- Owners of facilities are allowed to restrict use of facilities to themselves, their affiliates and other contracted parties.
- Contracts may be negotiated without regulatory oversight.
- Owners may charge market-based rates.

This policy is based on the FERC's determination that LNG facilities should be treated as part of the production sector rather than the pipeline sector. It should be noted that while these regulatory policies have been established for new facilities, more regulated policies remain in place for existing facilities built prior to the Hackberry Decision in 2002.

Offshore Facilities

In the U.S., the Department of Transportation (DOT) has jurisdiction for the siting and operation of offshore LNG facilities in federal waters under the Deep Water Port Act[3]. The DOT has delegated authority for review of all aspects of offshore facilities to the Coast Guard and Maritime Administration (MARAD). MARAD is the license issuing authority while the Coast Guard takes the lead on the application review and has primary responsibility for permitting which includes review of design, equipment and operations. In processing applications, the Coast Guard and MARAD must comply with the National Environmental Policy Act in reviewing the environmental impact of offshore facilities. Also reviewed are safety and security, with final authorization required by the Secretary of the DOT. Under current U.S. law, owners of offshore LNG facilities are not required to provide for open access and are allowed to charge market-based rates, thus giving these facilities equivalent terms-of-service and rate treatment to new onshore facilities. One additional key agency in the offshore process is the Department of the Interior's Minerals Management Service (MMS), which handles rights-of-way and hazard survey issues.

States also play a key role in permitting a deepwater port and related facilities. Since a deepwater port is outside state waters, most state participation is focused on the pipeline that will bring the gas to shore (such as the state's role in issuing a Coastal Zone Management Act consistency determination). However, the Deepwater Port Act also requires that the governor of the adjacent coastal state approve the port.

---

[3] The Deepwater Port Act applies to natural gas terminals located beyond state seawall boundaries. The Submerged Lands Act limits the seawall boundaries of the states to three geographical miles, except in the Gulf of Mexico where the limit is three marine leagues (about nine miles).

While the siting jurisdiction is clear, the states, through various state agencies, continue to play an important role in the permitting process. The Energy Policy Act specifically references the states' permitting authority under the Coastal Zone Management Act, the Clean Air Act and the Clean Water Act. A state agency properly exercising authority under one of these acts could effectively veto a proposed offshore LNG project.

Regulation of offshore LNG terminals is still developing in other countries since the concept is relatively new. Permitting is usually handled by a combination of federal agencies responsible for energy, the environment and shipping. As with shipping, international certification organizations are developing defined standards for design and construction of offshore facilities.

Permitting

Permitting of new facilities can be a long and difficult process given concerns over safety, security, land use, environmental impacts, and effects on gas markets. It is not uncommon for this process to take three or more years to complete. Permits are almost always reviewed and issued by federal agencies although in some countries local jurisdictions may also be required to approve the facilities. Issues that are generally considered include:

- The need for the new project and whether the project will provide benefits to the national economy and energy users.
- Facility design and operational procedures from the standpoint of safety, security and environmental impact.
- Facility location from the standpoint of safety, security, environmental impact, and land-use issues.

> **TYPICAL ENVIRONMENTAL IMPACT ISSUES**
>
> - Geological hazards
> - Soils and sediments
> - Water resources
> - Wetlands
> - Vegetation
> - Wildlife and aquatic resources
> - Threatened, endangered and other special status species
> - Land use, recreation and visual resources
> - Socioeconomics
> - Cultural resources
> - Air quality and noises
> - Safety issues
> - Terrorism and security issues
> - Necessary pipeline facilities
> - Cumulative impacts and recommended mitigation of them

SECTION SEVEN: REGULATION AND PERMITTING

- Regulation of open access, pricing and terms-of-service.

In the U.S., The Energy Policy Act of 2005 laid out specific regulatory responsibilities for review of new onshore LNG terminals. Similar regulation applies to offshore terminals although these are regulated by different agencies as described above. The Energy Policy Act of 2005 considers the terminals to be part of the competitive production sector rather than the more heavily regulated pipeline sector. Other key principles include:

- FERC has exclusive authority to approve or deny an application for the siting, construction, expansion, or operation of an LNG facility.

- Projects are reviewed under the Natural Gas Act Section 3, which requires only that FERC find the project is in the public interest (as opposed to pipeline reviews which are usually reviewed under Section 7, and require a more stringent determination that a project is necessary).

- Parties mutually agree to rates and terms and conditions of service that are not subject to regulatory oversight.

- Project owners are not required to offer open access or maintain a tariff and rate schedules.

- FERC must obtain concurrence from the Secretary of Defense prior to approval of any LNG facilities that may affect military installations.

- FERC is given exclusive authority to enforce environmental regulations with the states given only an advisory role.

Owners wishing to build a new onshore LNG facility must file an application with FERC well in advance of the desired construction date. The review process includes an Environmental Impact Statement (EIS) and in addition to environmental impact, considers safety and security issues as well as the potential public benefits that the project may provide. Key areas reviewed include:

- Adverse environmental impacts and how these could be mitigated.
- Alternatives to the proposed project.
- Engineering design and construction procedures.
- Economics of the project and its impacts on gas markets.
- Safety issues and how the applicant will address them.

- Security issues and how the applicant will address them.
- Regulatory factors such as effects on downstream pipelines.

In addition to the EIS, FERC also develops a separate cryogenic design review that considers technical design and operation plans to assure safe and reliable design and operations. The review process includes input from federal, state and local government agencies as well as members of the public and other interested organizations. This process generally takes at least two years and results in either rejection of the project or a finding that it provides public benefits. If approved, the order will contain various conditions that must be satisfied prior to construction. If denied, the applicant may be able to revise the application and reapply.

Although we have focused on the U.S. permitting process in this Section, similar procedures apply in other countries. Specific procedures depend on each country's environmental, safety and land-use planning laws.

What you will learn:

- The traditional structure of the LNG value chain
- How the value chain has evolved in recent years
- Who market participants are
- The structure of contracts throughout the value chain
- The risks that LNG market participants are exposed to and how they manage them
- How LNG projects are financed
- The current state of the market

SECTION EIGHT: MARKET DYNAMICS

The LNG industry has experienced impressive growth over its history, nearly doubling in size each decade between 1970 and 2010. Although international pipeline trade has also shown robust growth, LNG has increased its share of the global gas market from 10% in 1975 to over 28% in 2008. This strong growth has been driven by declining cost of capital, strong world demand, abundant worldwide stranded gas reserves, proven safety and reliability, and solid financial returns. As a result, we have also seen significant changes in contract structure and market dynamics.

The LNG Value Chain

The LNG value chain consists of:

- Natural gas production fields.
- A pipeline that delivers gas to the liquefaction plant.
- A liquefaction plant that provides processing, liquefaction and ship-loading.
- A fleet of LNG tankers.
- A regasification plant that includes ship off-loading, storage and regasification.
- A pipeline that delivers gas to large consumers, an interstate pipeline or directly to a gas utility's local distribution system.
- The local distribution system that delivers gas to consumers.

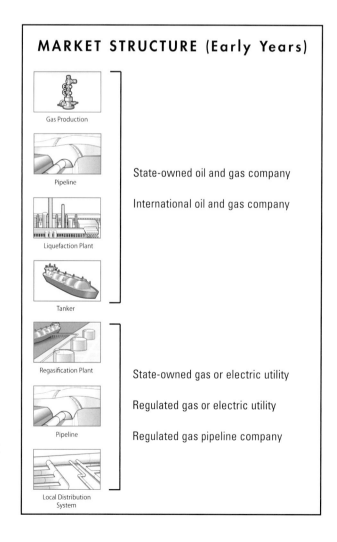

SECTION EIGHT: MARKET DYNAMICS

Prior to the 1990s the traditional model for the LNG marketplace consisted of just two segments: an upstream seller's consortium that provided gas production, liquefaction and shipping and a downstream buyer that provided regasification and delivery to the ultimate gas consumer (see illustration on page 87). The risks, both commercial and technical, involved in developing the early LNG value chain were perceived to be higher. This resulted in a conservative approach to business model development and a simple market structure.

Consortium ownership was mostly limited to state-owned or major international oil and gas companies. The consortium generally acted as a single entity for marketing purposes so that there was not competition among various owners of reserves. The buyers generally were state-controlled and/or regulated gas or electric utilities in Europe and Asia, or gas pipeline companies with long-term sales agreements to gas utilities in the U.S. With essentially one buyer and one seller, transactions were relatively simple.

In the absence of a long-term contractual commitment between the buying group and the selling group, projects were not constructed. Speculative development was not a viable option for participants or financiers since project economics depended on long-term uninterrupted delivery and sales. Multiyear contracts, typically 20 years or longer, minimized project investors' risk by providing a guaranteed cash flow to repay the amount borrowed and provide a reasonable return. Historically, contract terms were inflexible with little consideration for shifts in market demand. Even if economics favored diversion of ship volumes to other locations, the traditional long-term point-to-point trade model was built on factors that prevented flexibility. Some of these factors included dedicated shipping, buyer need for security of supply including right-of-first refusal on any additional production, buyer's ability to pass through the LNG cost to the end-use customer, lack of surplus liquefaction capacity, lack of market transparency and price signals, and the high cost of entry combined with the need for governmental approval.

The early 1990s saw the first evolution in the marketplace towards more short-term arrangements. Surplus LNG production in Indonesia caused state-owned Pertamina to develop innovative spot deals to monetize their excess production. These deals introduced time of delivery and volume flexibility with no take-or-pay provisions. They set the stage for further innovation.

Later in the decade new circumstances changed the market further. The Asian financial crisis dampened the need for supply in the world's largest buying region. At the

UNDERSTANDING TODAY'S GLOBAL LNG BUSINESS

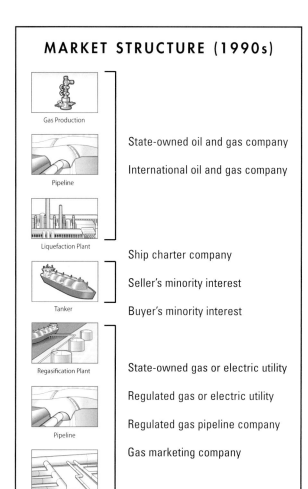

MARKET STRUCTURE (1990s)

same time, new liquefaction projects came on line to serve that market. During the same period on the other side of the world, European demand increased while supply was constricted from Algeria. In an unprecedented move, some of the LNG was diverted from Asia and rerouted to European and American markets. A cargo from Bontang, Indonesia was shipped to Boston in the first ever true spot transaction.

Also in the 1990s, new laws in the U.S., the U.K. and other European countries led to deregulation or liberalization, which resulted in unbundling of gas supply from distribution. This in turn led to European buyers demanding more flexibility in both new and renewed LNG contracts to match changes occurring in their gas markets. Under the traditional model, LNG buyers made money using their distribution assets to deliver regasified LNG, as natural gas, to customers. So end-use customers bore the entire cost of the gas, regardless of the price level. As the laws changed, and regional indigenous supply prices diverged from the cost of LNG, customers and regulators were no longer content to absorb the higher costs of LNG. With changing regulation, LNG purchased under long-term inflexible agreements no longer matched market needs. For regasification facilities treated as regulated assets, the new rules also required the provision of open access services to multiple market participants at a regulated tariff rate. Participants, including non-traditional parties such as gas marketers, began seeing the LNG value chain in a different light. Looking at each piece of the chain independently brought a shift in the shipping role and its potential for profits. This led to control of shipping moving away from just the sellers. New shipping consortia emerged which included upstream and downstream participants as well as the traditional shipping firms. These consortia moved the industry away from a model where tankers were dedicated to a specific project to one in which a tanker offered flexible transportation options between multiple upstream providers and downstream buyers. During this time we also began to see a blurring of the line between buyer and seller. Buyers expanded their positions further upstream by becoming minority partners in upstream projects, while sellers, through natural gas marketing affiliates, began to expand downstream into regasification.

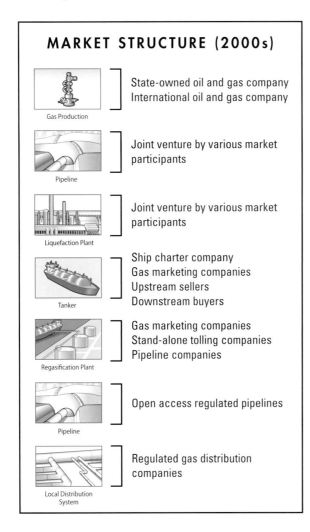

As the market moved into the 2000s (see illustration to the left), the LNG business has become even more fragmented and fluid with downstream market participants becoming more involved upstream, upstream participants becoming involved downstream, multiple producers competing to provide supply to liquefaction plants, various market participants investing in LNG tankers, and stand-alone liquefaction and regasification facilities providing tolling services[1]. While the value chain continues to evolve into a more fragmented market structure, it should be noted that most existing projects as well as some of the newer projects are still following the more integrated structures from earlier times.

Market Participants

The evolution of the LNG marketplace mirrors an evolution in the participants who buy, sell and ship LNG. The original sellers' consortia in the 1970s and 1980s were dominated by national oil companies such as Sonatrach (Algeria), Pertamina (Indonesia) and Petronas (Malaysia), often in partnership with major oil and gas companies such as Exxon, BP and Shell. Buyers were mostly large utilities such as Gaz de France (France), Tokyo Gas (Japan), Chubu Electric (Japan), and Korea Gas (South Korea). In the U.S., buyers were pipelines companies (such as Columbia Gas, El Paso and Southern Trunkline), with long-term contracts to sell gas supply to utilities.

---

[1] Tolling refers to liquefaction and/or regasification that is provided to market participants for a contracted fee.

In the 2000s, a significant change occurred in market participants – both in the number of countries entering the marketplace (buying and selling) and in the types of entities involved. New or expanded liquefaction and regasification terminals have brought numerous new entities and countries into the LNG marketplace. While national oil companies are still important in the upstream sector, the role of the major oil and gas companies (BP, Chevron, ExxonMobil, Shell and TotalFinaElf) as well as smaller or regional producers/marketers (BG, ConocoPhillips, Repsol, Tractebel/Suez, and Statoil) has expanded downstream. Additionally, in an effort to increase flexibility and mitigate risks, a number of downstream partners have taken partial ownership in liquefaction facilities (Kogas, Tepco, Tokyo Gas, Japanese trading houses such as Mitsubishi and Mitsui, and CNOOC). Participation is even more diverse in downstream facilities, at least in the competitive markets of North America and Europe. Proposed participants in these markets range from the oil and gas majors and smaller regional producers/marketers listed above to utilities (Gaz de France, National Grid and Transco), pipeline companies (Enbridge, TransCanada), merchant generators (AES), merchant regasification plant owners (Cheniere, Excelerate Energy) and integrated regional utilities/marketers (Dominion Resources, Sempra Energy). Ownership in the shipping sector has also exploded with ship owners now ranging from upstream producers to marketing companies, downstream buyers, and a few stand-alone shipping companies (Golar LNG, Exmar and Maran).

Contract Structure

Prior to the 1990s, the central contract for LNG projects was the Sales Purchase Agreement (SPA). Since projects were developed as an integrated chain, the SPA covered most transactions from the liquefaction plant through the point of sale into the regasification terminal. Another key agreement was the joint venture agreement between members of the sellers' consortium. Agreements on the buyers' side were not generally required since each buyer simply regasified and sold the gas as part of its overall utility gas merchant function.

The evolution of market structure has added considerable complexity in contracting. As more participants become involved, the need for more complex contracts grows because the natural gas (in both gaseous and LNG form) may change hands a number of times between the producer and the ultimate consumer. These other parties, such as shippers and liquefaction and regasification facility owners, will need separate contracts for each service provided.

SECTION EIGHT: MARKET DYNAMICS

> **KEY PROVISIONS OF A SALES PURCHASE AGREEMENT**
>
> - The point of sale
> - Price and any provisions for price reopeners
> - Length of contract
> - Contractual quantity
> - Take-or-pay provisions
> - Penalties for failure to perform
> - Destination clauses
> - Force majeure provisions
> - Provisions for who is responsible for various costs through the value chain (such as insurance, shipping, taxes, etc.).

Under the traditional market structure, SPAs covered long terms – usually up to 25 years. The contracts typically involved very specific take-or-pay provisions with annual contract quantities. Pricing was primarily indexed to oil or oil-related market prices. A price floor was often included to protect owners of the liquefaction facilities from selling below costs. The total output from liquefaction plants was often contracted to only one or two buyers. Shipping services were typically provided under CIF (cost, insurance, freight) provisions with delivery ex-ship – meaning that the sellers were responsible for all costs to the tanker plus the cost of shipping and insuring the cargo until the ship reached the regasification terminal. Cargos were generally contracted to a specific buyer destination and could not be rerouted by either the seller or the buyer (due to very specific destination clauses within the ship charter and the SPA). Ownership transferred from seller to buyer as the gas was moved from the tanker to the regasification terminal. Contracts were generally between stable and large entities, often backed by government ownership and/or regulated ratepayers. Thus counterparty risks were low.

As the marketplace began evolving in the 1990s, short-term sales contracts and spot sales were introduced. While long-term agreements with take-or-pay and oil-indexed pricing still remained the norm for baseload amounts, many owners of liquefaction facilities developed capabilities to produce quantities of LNG in excess of initial design capacities. The result was a new wave of short-term and spot contracts designed to market these excess quantities. These contracts tended to do away with take-or-pay provisions and rather defined a specific quantity of LNG at a specific price over a limited period of time. As the shipping business became disaggregated from the sellers' consortia, many contracts specified delivery FOB (freight on board), meaning that LNG ownership changed hands at the outlet of the liquefaction terminal. Shipping costs were often covered through charter agreements with ship owners and were paid by the buyer. Credit risk still remained relatively low as volumes not locked into long-

UNDERSTANDING TODAY'S GLOBAL LNG BUSINESS

TYPICAL LNG PRICING

Traditional Market Structure

Asia: Japanese import index for crude oil ("Japanese crude cocktail")

Europe: Fuel oil index for European ports

North America: Base price plus increase tied to inflation and crude oil index

2000s

Asia: Japanese crude cocktail adjusted by an S-curve

Europe: Natural gas price index at National Balancing Point (U.K.) or Zeebrugge Hub (Belgium)

North America: Natural gas price index at Henry Hub

---

term agreements were generally small and insurance could be purchased against loss of cargo during shipping.

With the emergence of the disaggregated marketplace of the 2000s, contractual terms have become even more complex and the number of contracts required for the complete value chain has grown. Some existing contracts have been partially renegotiated to reflect current market conditions. Areas typically changed include modification of crude-related pricing equations (to provide more stable LNG pricing in the event of oil price volatility), flexibility in destination and flexibility in take-or-pay arrangements (allowing volumes to more closely reflect market needs or timing on deliveries). Much of this contract flexibility has been inspired by deregulation of the downstream sector which has allowed both sup-

---

LNG SWAPS

More flexibility in the natural gas marketplace can provide an opportunity for market participants to reduce their overall transportation costs by agreeing to swap LNG cargos. For example, suppose that one gas marketer has a contract to deliver Trinidadian supply to Europe while a second marketer has a contract to deliver Algerian supply to the U.S. A quick look at the map will show that the overall cost of LNG transportation, which is usually a daily charter rate, could be reduced by simply redirecting the tankers to the markets that are closest to the supply sources, thus reducing the number of days a ship is chartered.

As might be expected, such a transaction is easier said than done. Contractual details and sharing of benefits must be worked out between sellers, buyers and shippers involved, and other issues may arise relating to tanker compatibility with port facilities, facility availability, and gas specifications for local markets. But where possible, swaps can result in significant reductions in transportation costs.

SECTION EIGHT: MARKET DYNAMICS

KEY CONTRACT CLAUSES

Pricing – A description of how the price will be set at any point in time. Usually indexed to the price of an alternate fuel or alternate supply source and may include ceilings, floors or an S-curve provision.

Take-or-pay – A provision that requires the buyer to pay for a certain volume of LNG whether or not the buyer actually takes delivery of that volume.

Destination Clauses – A contractual restriction on the destination of cargos and which party controls the choice of destination. An alternative is destination flexibility, with potential economic benefit to the seller if an alternate destination is chosen.

Delivery Point – Specification of the delivery point.

Scheduling of Deliveries – Specification of the timing for deliveries from liquefaction facilities and ships as well as provisions covering who is responsible for delays.

Handling of Boil-off – Specification of who is responsible for the loss of volumes due to boil-off.

Heat Rate – Specification of the heat rate for the delivered LNG and who is responsible for the costs of any processing required to get the gas to the necessary specifications for delivery via the pipeline and/or distribution system.

Force Majeure – A description of what events excuse a party from performance without penalty.

Liabilities – A description of remedies for failure of one party to perform absent a force majeure event. This may include provisions for liquidated damages or other defined liabilities.

Financial Security/Guarantees – A description of who is responsible for liabilities in the event of default. Parties specified are typically parent or affiliated companies. In the absence of parental guarantees, the contract may specify that parties take out a letter of credit, execute performance bonds or deposit money into escrow to back their performance guarantees. This provision may also allow for the "aggrieved" party to take over the role of the defaulting party in the project. In other cases, governmental agencies or government-backed banks may provide security guarantees.

Termination Rights – A description of when a party is allowed to terminate the agreement. Circumstances triggering the right to terminate may include satisfaction of specific obligations to deliver and/or take, failure of the other party to perform, an extended force majeure condition, or a significant decline in the financial position of one party.

Dispute Settlement and Governing Law – Since almost all agreements are international, the parties must clearly specify how disputes will be settled and under what legal authority the agreement will be governed.

pliers and buyers to participate in short-term, spot and swap markets. Contracts for new projects now reflect the disaggregation of the marketplace and include some or all of the following:

- Production sharing agreements in the gas fields between various resource equity owners.

- A sales agreement between the lead gas producer and a gas marketer who will take ownership of LNG at the outlet of the liquefaction terminal and sell either LNG or regasified natural gas to a downstream market.

- A tariff arrangement between the producers and the feed-gas pipeline.

- A tolling agreement between the producers and the owner of the liquefaction plant for liquefaction and loading of the LNG onto the tanker.

- A ship charter agreement between the ship owner and the LNG owner.

- A tolling agreement between the gas marketer and the owner of the regasification terminal for off-loading, storage and regasification.

- A tariff arrangement between the gas marketer and the transmission pipeline.

- A sales agreement between the gas marketer and the utility or end-use customer purchasing the gas.

- Plus an additional number of agreements if new facilities will be constructed, including financing and shareholder agreements, engineering and construction agreements, and ongoing operation and maintenance agreements for the facility.

As the global marketplace for LNG becomes more robust, there will be more sales or swaps of LNG cargos or regasified volumes between marketers at various spots along the value chain, requiring additional changes to traditional LNG contracting practices. Owners of LNG liquefaction facilities and/or regasification terminals may also elect to contract different portions of their capacity to different parties. In some cases, regasification terminals may be required to offer their capacity to the marketplace under open access rules, meaning that the owners must hold an open season or other bidding process to give any market participant a fair opportunity to obtain capacity. However, in many parts of the world (including the U.S.) regulators have allowed regasification owners the right to contract capacity privately, without going through the open access process.

LNG sales agreements for today's projects providing supply to Europe or North America are much more likely to have prices indexed to alternate natural gas supply

SECTION EIGHT: MARKET DYNAMICS

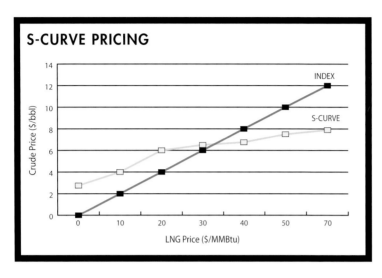

sources (such as natural gas hub index prices in the U.S. and in Europe) and may include floors that represent alternate supply prices (such as the Russian Gazprom gas sales price in Europe). Sales agreements for supply to Asia still tend to be tied to the Japanese crude price, although the use of S-curves – as an alternative to index pricing – to dampen out extreme price volatility is common (see illustration above). Most agreements have more flexible take-or-pay arrangements than in the past. While contracts for minimum firm off-take may be necessary to finance a liquefaction facility, liquefaction owners are now much more likely to move forward with projects not fully contracted. This is primarily due to robust global markets which provide an opportunity to sell excess volumes at a potentially higher spot price. An additional factor is the size of the new facilities. Few buyers have the demand to absorb all the volume from a megatrain such as Sakhalin or the new Qatar plants. Take-or-pay provisions may also include the flexibility for make-up cargos at later dates since LNG suppliers have greater opportunities to market volumes that aren't taken at a specific time. Single destination clauses are much less likely to appear in current agreements as well since marketers and downstream regulators desire the flexibility to re-route cargos to locations where they are most valuable.

Short-term and spot contracts are a new breed of agreement that have gained popularity in recent years. In these agreements, provisions such as take-or-pay are not likely to be included and pricing may be at a specific negotiated price rather than at an index. Often parties will negotiate a master agreement that includes standard terms and conditions, then simply add purchase orders for each individual sale that cover specific details such as price, quantity and destination.

Risk Management in the LNG Marketplace

Because LNG projects now depend on the performance of a number of parties located in multiple countries, the risk potential is very high. Each sector of the LNG industry faces its own unique set of risks. These include the following:

- Gas supply — Risks relate to the certainty that gas supply will be available at an acceptable price to make a project viable. As you have learned, a successful LNG project requires low-cost gas supply that will last for at least the time required to pay off any loans and make an acceptable rate of return on the project. As larger projects become standard, more than one production field may be required to fill plant capacity. When the supply is developed is also important since the timing of development and production must match liquefaction plant construction. Performance guarantees from the producers are often necessary to cover this risk.

> **RISKS IN THE LNG MARKETPLACE**
>
> **Supply** – The risk that expected supplies will be unavailable at an acceptable price.
>
> **Construction** – The risk that construction issues will result in project delays or increased project capital costs.
>
> **Operational** – The risk that operational problems will result in interruptions of supply or an increase in operating costs.
>
> **Price** – The risk of adverse price changes.
>
> **Volume** – The risk that volumes purchased by the market will be lower than expected.
>
> **Political** – The risk that actions of governmental bodies will change the project fundamentals. Actions that might occur include expropriation, oppressive taxation or interruption of contractual provisions.
>
> **Regulatory** – The risk that regulators will change the rules associated with project terms and conditions. Regulatory risk is usually associated with the buyer's country and may include deregulation (also known as liberalization in some parts of the world), reregulation and changes to existing regulatory standards (such as ratemaking, open access rules and environmental regulations).
>
> **Counterparty** – The risk that a contractual counterparty will fail to perform.

- Liquefaction — A primary risk is the completion time of the project. Since revenue does not come in until the project is complete and operational, financing must be provided through construction and start-up. The failure to bring construction in on time and on budget could result in escalating interest costs and the financial instability of the project. A common solution is to require a turn-key fixed-price construction contract where the risk of time delays and cost overruns is placed on the contractor. The result of this solution is that only the largest international construction companies have the financial wherewithal to participate. After commercial operation, risks include operational risks and the potential for higher than expected operating costs.

- Shipping — Risks include availability of ships, timing on construction of new ships, operational risks, technology risks, and political risks associated with not only the liquefaction and regasification countries but also any regions through which the ship must travel. To mitigate these risks, insurance is necessary and construction contracts are awarded only to proven shipbuilders.

- Regasification — Risks are similar to those associated with liquefaction with the added regulatory risk associated with terms and conditions of service that may be changed by regulators within the host country.

- Downstream markets – Downstream risks include price, volume and regulatory risk. Price risk relates to the market price of gas in the buyers' area and volume risk relates to enough demand in the buyers' area to absorb the gas. These risks were traditionally covered by long-term SPAs. Such agreements were signed by creditworthy buyers and included take-or-pay provisions at indexed prices as well as price floors sufficient to cover project costs. As we move into a marketplace where spot pricing is common, lenders and equity owners must look for new ways to handle price risk – perhaps through long-term agreements for minimum supply volumes and/or the use of financial instruments to hedge prices. Regulatory risk is also a factor in downstream markets since buyers are often regulated utilities and a change in regulation may affect their ability to meet contractual obligations.

TYPICAL CAPITAL COSTS FOR NEW LNG DELIVERY CHAIN DEVELOPMENT

Exploration and Production	Liquefaction	Shipping	Regasification
$0.5 to $1.5 billion	$1 to $2 billion	$0.4 to $2 billion	$0.5 to $1.5 billion

Financing LNG Projects

Because of the large capital investment required to build LNG infrastructure, financing is a critical component of the overall business. Financial arrangements for LNG facilities generally include a mix of loans and equity investment. Lenders make a profit through interest paid on the debt, while equity investors normally profit through dividends and/or an increase in the value of their ownership stake. In the case of LNG facilities, an equity investor may also profit by leveraging its investment to obtain capacity in the facility. Returns can then be realized through the marketing of gas. Lenders and investors weigh the risk of a project by determining the likelihood that actual returns will vary from the expected return. Traditionally, LNG projects have been considered relatively low risk due to the certainty of positive cash flow supported by long-term agreements with creditworthy parties and take-or-pay provisions. This has allowed LNG projects to be financed at high debt/equity ratios (sometimes as high as 90% debt) and relatively low interest rates. With traditional structures in flux, lenders and equity participants are now much more careful about investing in a project. The result has been that many new projects are internally financed by industry partners. Such entities may be more comfortable with the inherent risk since it is already part of their primary business.

Financing of LNG projects occurs in three stages:

- Development financing — This covers the stage prior to governmental approval and start of construction. This stage is highly risky since many projects will never achieve approvals or move to construction. The investment cost, which is generally $5 to $15 million, is entirely at risk if the project fails to go forward. On

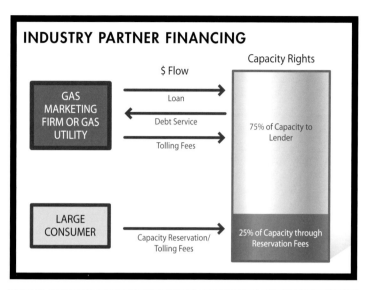

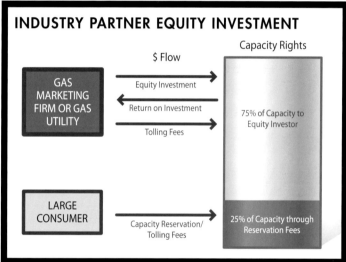

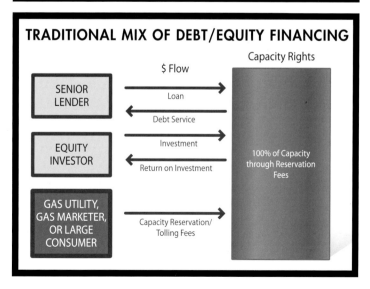

the flip side, potential return can reach ten times the investment or more. Large energy companies often finance development from their own balance sheet (i.e. with shareholders dollars), while independent developers generally seek financing from venture capital firms or high net worth individuals.

- Construction financing — This covers the stage between start of construction and movement into commercial operation. Funding needs vary by project size and design, but requirements of at least $700 million are not uncommon. There are two different approaches to construction financing. One is a combination of debt and shareholder equity that is secured by long-term agreement with terminal users. The second is industry partner financing where an industry partner (gas marketer, gas utility and/or large consumer) finances the construction in exchange for capacity rights.

- Term financing — This is the long-term financing that pays off development and construction financing and provides ongoing working capital. Term financing needs may commonly be as high as $1 billion or more. Often the same entity that provided construction financing will roll the construction loan into a new term agreement. Common term financing strategies include industry partner financing, industry partner equity investments, and the more traditional mix of third-party debt and equity financing (see illustrations on page 99).

Prior to financing a project or participating in a project as an equity partner, market participants must carefully analyze the potential return and risks associated. Key issues include projected rate of return, the long-term availability of gas supply, long-term demand projections in the consuming market, the political and regulatory stability of the producing and buying countries, the availability of shipping, volumes covered by take-or-pay agreements, the creditworthiness of buyers, risk allocation between various participating parties, and the availability of security and/or guarantees. As you might imagine, investing in an LNG project is really limited to a select group of companies who not only understand the risks, but are also willing and able to accept them.

The Current State of the LNG Market

As of early 2010, the LNG marketplace was characterized by rapid growth and significant changes in the way that business is transacted, but with uncertainties driven by the economic downturn and the growth of shale gas production in the U.S. Key factors affecting the marketplace included:

- An increase in demand for natural gas in Europe and Asia, driven by environmental concerns in Europe and economic growth in Asian markets.

- Declining domestic production in Canada and the U.K., but increasing production in the U.S.

- The desire of European buyers for additional alternatives to pipeline-delivered gas from near-monopoly sellers.

- Uncertainty about future market prices for natural gas due to recent price volatility.

- Declining unit capital costs for liquefaction, shipping and regasification, partially offset by rising material and manpower costs.

- A disaggregation in delivery chains driven by downstream deregulation in the U.S. and Europe.

- A greater willingness by a number of consuming countries (including Mexico, the U.K., France, Spain, India, and China) to support the construction of new LNG terminals.

- The desire of a number of producing countries to use LNG as a means of monetizing natural gas assets or reducing environmental impacts (such as Nigerian projects supported by the need to discontinue flaring of natural gas).

- The need for the oil and gas majors to monetize new sources of worldwide gas and their willingness to invest in the development of LNG.

- The willingness of oil and gas majors, as well as regional gas producers/marketers to invest in or contractually commit to both upstream facilities and downstream regasification terminals.

That the LNG business is growing rapidly cannot be denied. Liquefaction capacity in the world grew by more than 80% in the decade between 1990 and 2000. For the decade beginning in 2000 this capacity will again increase substantially. So one key trend in today's marketplace is a frenzied pace of proposals for development of new facilities and a struggle to put in place new contractual agreements to support the financing of them. Given the demand needs in consuming countries in Asia and Europe, the LNG construction business is and will continue to be robust.

In North America, construction of new terminals has slowed to a crawl with the advent of new and lower-cost domestic sources of supply. However, construction still continues on terminals already under way prior to the fall of prices and the economic crisis in 2008/2009. Even though additional new construction may be very limited, over 30 proposals still remain announced and active, and many of these have already received approval from the appropriate federal agency.

Today's LNG business is also characterized by a continuing evolution in market structure and business practices. While much of the LNG business remains tied to traditional long-term contracts, even these projects are seeing renegotiation of contract terms to provide for more pricing and delivery flexibility. The faster pace of deregulation in Europe and North America has led to two distinct physical markets. In the Atlantic, short-term agreements and spot trading are becoming more common. This trend somewhat matches, although with a significant lag, the deregulation or liberalization of the pipeline and natural gas sales sectors of the industry in Europe and North America. In the more Asian dominated Pacific Basin, long-term contracts still predominate, although even these are being renegotiated to provide for more flexibility in pricing and take-or-pay arrangements. Instead of a single long-term contract covering the entire output, contracts are more likely to be tiered for portions of the output with different terms and lengths, including short-term, medium-term and long-term components.

While financing arrangements for new projects will likely continue to require a baseload of firm contractual commitments, projects are now being structured to allow some capacity dedicated to spot markets. The deregulation of downstream markets has also changed the character of market participants. While traditional projects were often anchored by a single downstream buyer who was either a national energy company or a regulated utility, deregulation has reduced the number and financial clout of such participants. In some countries, potential natural gas buyers have become a diverse group comprised of non-regulated retail marketers, large industrial consumers, merchant power producers, and wholesale gas traders. New projects are often anchored by major producers who are pushing downstream in the value chain since they are the only entities remaining in the marketplace with the financial wherewithal to pull together complete projects. These producers then act as gas marketers in the consuming country, selling the regasified volumes to end users, utilities and power generators.

These trends have also led to the rise of the "merchant" regasification terminal owner. Since it is now less feasible for downstream utilities to own and operate terminals, and producers may see this as their area of expertise, a new role has been opened for the regasification terminal owner who will operate as a tolling facility backed by long-term capacity agreements with upstream and downstream market participants. A similar new role has been opened in the shipping industry, where ship owners may no longer be tied to specific projects but can offer ship charters to whichever market provides for best returns.

As we move forward we expect to see continued evolution. We will consider the future of LNG in the next Section.

What you will learn:

- How the LNG business may continue to evolve

- Key technology, geopolitical and market issues

- A vision for the future of the global LNG business

SECTION NINE: THE FUTURE

As we look forward into the 21st century, projections for world energy consumption growth are staggering. Overall energy consumption is expected to grow by 33% between 2010 and 2030, with much of this growth fueled by natural gas[1]. Since many consuming regions are significantly distant from supply regions, the natural gas business has little choice but to evolve into one dominated by long-distance pipeline and LNG transport. LNG, which made up about 7.5% of world natural gas supply in 2008 has been forecast to make up as much as 18% of world trade by 2030[2]. At the same time, new sources of gas such as shale gas look promising as an alternative to LNG in some regions including the U.S. It is likely that the future LNG business will look very different from that of today. As the industry evolves, areas to watch include advancements in technology, geopolitics, alternate gas sources, and global natural gas markets.

Technology Issues

Much of today's cautious optimism about the future of LNG stems from the fact that LNG technology costs declined by over 30% during the 1990s. This drove the break-even point for LNG down to where it is competitive with supplies delivered by pipeline in some regions. Future technological developments may further reduce costs in the long run. In the short term, labor shortages and rising material costs for steel, concrete and nickel are putting upward cost pressure on projects currently underway. In addition, financing has become an issue with the worldwide credit crunch. The crisis will affect the approval of future projects and may cause construction just underway to be put on hold until a time of greater stability. However, the upward trend in LNG demand is expected to resume given growth in Asian demand and pressures in most markets to utilize natural gas as a cleaner fuel than coal or oil.

One area where producers hope to cut costs is through the development of larger and larger liquefaction trains, which has been fostered by the shift from steam-driven to

---

[1] Usage projections are from the EIA, *International Energy Outlook 2009*.

[2] Based on projections for overall world gas demand from Ibid and for world LNG trade from *LNG to 2030: A Detailed Review of Future Volumes and Trends*, August 2008, Ocean Shipping Consultants Limited.

SECTION NINE: THE FUTURE

gas turbine compressors. These mega-trains are in the process of being brought into production in Qatar as of early 2010. While it is hoped they will reduce costs by taking advantage of scale, the true benefits are yet unproven. Other cost savings may come from larger tankers and a move to on-board liquefaction facilities that can prevent loss through boil-off. In April 2009, RasGas delivered its first full Q-Flex LNG load to India and recently took delivery of their first Q-Max LNG tanker for use on this and other delivery routes. These ships include onboard reliquefaction plants, cutting cargo loss and thus reducing transport costs.

Meanwhile, development of offshore regasification technology may persuade nervous communities to allow regasification terminals to be sited. With regasification facilities located on board, tankers can be moored offshore and away from populous areas. The first of the offshore terminal buoys using Excelerate's Energy Bridge™ technology went into service in the Gulf of Mexico in 2005. There are now two additional terminals in operation to receive the regasified LNG directly from these specialized ships; one at a port location in the U.K. and another offshore facility in Massachusetts. Other offshore technologies are in use in Argentina, Brazil and Italy. While costs for offshore regasification are higher, this technology may allow for regasification near major markets such as California and the Northeast U.S., which have so far resisted local siting of regasification terminals. Some industry participants envision a future where a fleet of regasification vessels could be used to flexibly deliver gas to any number of consumer markets based on specific market needs and price fluctuations.

While gas-to-liquids (GTL) conversion technology is different from the technology used to produce LNG, it may also have future impacts on the LNG marketplace. GTL converts natural gas to a liquid fuel that can be transported and refined in a similar fashion as crude oil. The resulting synthetic fuels burn more cleanly than petroleum-based fuels and can be transported more cheaply than LNG. GTL projects are being pursued by major oil and gas companies such as Exxon and Shell and over time may become an alternate path to market for large natural gas reserves. As of early 2010, there were 34 GTL plants operational, under construction, or announced worldwide. While most of these facilities are located in the Middle East or Africa, future facilities may be constructed in Asia, Australia, South American, and Alaska. Although it is conceivable that future development of a GTL industry could result in both competition for LNG and a reduction in available reserves, it appears that any such impacts will be seen in the longer term. Even so, the development of GTL technologies certainly should be closely watched by anyone interested in LNG.

The last key technology advancement that is sure to have strong impact on the LNG marketplace is improvement in electric generation technology. In many parts of the world, combined-cycle gas turbines have become the favored technology due to low capital costs of construction, rapid deployment, operational flexibility, environmental benefits, and higher efficiencies in converting fuel to electricity. The future market for LNG will partially depend on the competitive position of gas-fired generation relative to other fuel sources such as coal, nuclear and renewables.

Geopolitical Issues

The future direction of the LNG marketplace will also be strongly impacted by regulatory and political developments. Issues to watch include whether local community concerns result in delays or cancellation of proposed regasification terminals; whether regulatory bodies will treat terminals as open access cost-based regulated assets or whether they will allow owners to negotiate access terms and charge market-based prices; and whether deregulation of downstream sectors in Asia will result in changes similar to those that have occurred in Europe and North America. Also important will be future environmental regulations. The implementation of carbon emissions regulations tends to favor gas-fired electricity generation since carbon emissions from gas are about one-half that of coal. The Kyoto Protocol has already brought carbon emissions regulations and carbon credit trading to Canada, Europe, Russia, and Japan, but important consuming countries including the U.S., China and India are not yet involved. And although the future of carbon emission regulation was still being debated in early 2010, it appeared that carbon emissions would eventually be regulated in all major world economies. Future growth of carbon regulations and carbon credit trading should foster growth in gas demand and a corresponding demand for LNG.

Political developments merit monitoring as well. Much of the world's natural gas supply is located in regions such as the Middle East, Africa, Indonesia, Russia, and Venezuela where long-term political stability is uncertain. Instability in some or all of these regions could harm the growth of the LNG business. Many observers have also pointed out that LNG facilities (liquefaction terminals, tankers and regasification terminals) may become the target of terrorist activities. So a rise in terrorism could put a damper on the LNG business. On the flip side, a growth in LNG imports can also allow a country to diversify its sources of supply. For instance Spain has developed LNG as an alternative to over-dependence on pipeline imports from Algeria, while other parts of Europe view LNG as an opportunity to avoid over-dependence on Russian supplies. Twice in the last few years Russia has held up gas deliveries to downstream buyers while

SECTION NINE: THE FUTURE

price disputes were resolved. LNG as an alternate and flexible supply reduces the capability of any one producing region to determine prices. The supply diversity provided by LNG also lessens risks of supply interruptions and price spikes.

Lastly there is a real and valid concern that further development of the LNG marketplace will increase consuming countries' dependence on imported energy supply and will simply exacerbate issues already experienced in the oil marketplace. Talk has even arisen about the possibility of a future gas producers' organization – similar to oil's OPEC – that could work to coordinate production levels and support specific LNG price targets. The Gas Exporting Countries Forum (GECF), formed in 2001, is a loosely tied group of gas producers seeking to represent and push their mutual interests. Members in early 2010 included Algeria, Bolivia, Egypt, Equatorial Guinea, Iran, Kazakhstan (as an observer) Libya, Nigeria, Norway (as an observer), Qatar, Russia, Trinidad and Tobago, and Venezuela. Together these countries represent over 65% of the world's gas reserves and close to 40% of gas production. Fortunately for consuming countries, there are many barriers to the development of a large producers' cartel in natural gas including the diversity of membership, the increasing interrelationship between ownership of upstream and downstream sectors, the existence of numerous long-term contracts with indexed pricing, the small role LNG plays in setting gas prices in the consuming markets of Europe and the U.S., and the difficulty that would be experienced in trying to agree on production quotas. However, the evolution of this organization bears watching as smaller groups of countries including Iran and Russia have discussed ways to create an organization that could influence world production and pricing.

Current supply/demand projections suggest that the major economies of Europe and Asia have little choice but to increase their dependence on imported natural gas. While politicians always like to talk about energy self-sufficiency, the truth is it just isn't reality. Many major consuming countries have really just two options: learning to accept significant increases in imported LNG or learning to use less natural gas. And most economies of the world simply don't appear interested in learning to use less natural gas any time soon.

Market Issues

Where then will LNG markets go in the future? Markets have a funny habit of evolving in ways that defy prediction. So we'll leave market predictions to the psychics. But following are some key questions whose answers are sure to affect future market evolution:

Will LNG Demand Continue to Grow?

The demand for LNG is driven by various factors including natural gas production rates in consuming markets (notably Canada, the U.S. and Europe), the competitiveness of natural gas transported by pipeline, and overall demand for natural gas. Current projections indicate that growth in production rates will continue to decline in Canada and Northern Europe and that the costs of maintaining existing production rates will escalate. But new finds or exploration technology could change this. For instance, the expectation of future production available in the U.S. has recently dramatically changed as new shale gas finds boost reserves. For many markets, the cost of expanding natural gas supplies via pipeline appears high. In Asia, a pipeline from Turkmenistan to China was recently opened and there has been talk of constructing pipelines from Iran to India and from Russia to either China, Korea or Japan. One or more of these projects may get built, but certainly there are a myriad of political issues to be covered first and costs will be significant. Each major pipeline project built will reduce the market for LNG, or at least put pressure on commodity pricing.

Despite the recent volatility of natural gas prices in Europe and the U.S., it still appears that overall natural gas demand will grow in these markets following the global economic recovery, and that it will also grow rapidly in developing countries of the world, especially China and India. Although extreme scenarios can be contemplated where rapid growth in supply located near markets could dampen demand for LNG, it appears likely that much of the future demand growth will be served by LNG.

Will Investment Be Available to Construct the Necessary Infrastructure?

The projected growth in LNG markets is estimated to require an infrastructure investment of as much as $400 billion. The current deregulated marketplace in many downstream countries puts the burden of financing these projects (or in committing to sufficient long-term contracts to convince bankers to finance them) increasingly on shareholders of private companies rather than on national governments or on regulated entities that can finance projects on the backs of their ratepayers. Private companies will continually reevaluate whether investments in LNG are the best use of their money. While credit is tighter now due to the world financial crisis, governments and large integrated energy companies still have the funding to continue financing LNG assets. The question remains whether or not these assets are viewed as the right investment to secure energy sources or monetize energy assets. And just a few unfortunate shocks (e.g., a major accident, a successful terrorist attack, an LNG-related business failure, or a global financial meltdown) could rapidly change this picture. But at least for now, it appears the need for producing countries to monetize gas assets and for consuming countries to ensure access to supply will result in continued investment in LNG.

How Will the LNG Business Adapt to Short-term Markets?

While much of the LNG world still works on long-term agreements within an integrated value chain, much of the consuming world in both natural gas and electricity generation is becoming more and more accustomed to short-term markets and spot trading. While a five-year gas agreement may seem like a long-term deal to a gas consumer in New York or London, it looks like a very short-term deal to the financier of a $2 billion dollar plus LNG investment. Some observers have argued that long-term physical contracts can be replaced by financial instruments used to manage risk. Certainly this evolution has worked for gas producers in the North American market who use financial instruments to finance exploration and production activities. But most currently available instruments are not good matches for the risks relative to the LNG marketplace, and evolution of global financial instruments would be required. In the meantime the market will struggle to find a balance between longer and shorter deals, and in some cases, LNG development may be slowed by a lack of investors with large enough balance sheets to carry the risk of major projects.

It appears that LNG projects at new sites will still largely be financed with long-term contracts due to the necessary capital and length of time required to develop the project. Short-term contracts may become the norm for projects whose capital investment has already been recovered.

How Will Future Prices Be Determined?

LNG prices have traditionally been indexed to oil-based alternative fuels, but in North America and Europe they are increasingly indexed to local natural gas prices. Indexing in local markets tends to push price risk back to the producer since low prices benefit only the buyer and high-priced volumes can be resold in the spot market, in essence cancelling out the buyers' obligations (and risk). Producers then face the prospect of being stuck with uneconomic netbacks when prices fall in the consuming countries. Meanwhile, electric generators may want prices indexed to alternative fuels such as coal or nuclear generation. The ultimate pricing paradigm will determine a lot about the risks of developing new projects and will have a strong impact on future LNG market growth.

Who Will Dominate the Future Marketplace?

As noted previously, the growth of the LNG business will require both huge capital investments and organizations capable of navigating the difficult waters of international politics and regulations. Ideal for many consumers might be a highly competitive marketplace characterized by liquid markets, transparent market-based pricing and high levels of competition. Perhaps more likely is a business dominated by a few large major players who are the only ones capable of making the financial commitments and managing a myriad of risks. The next few years will prove an interesting time as governments, national oil companies, oil and gas majors, regional gas companies, and consumers grapple for a competitive edge in this developing marketplace.

Global Gas

Even with the uncertainties noted above, let's go out on a limb and suggest a vision for the future of LNG. As we move further into the 21st century it is likely that a natural gas business depending on long-distance pipeline and LNG tanker transport will become the primary energy business in global commerce. While the oil business will struggle with environmental issues and the need to grow production sufficiently to avoid huge price increases, the natural gas industry will likely be able to fuel growing demands while reducing environmental impacts of energy consumption and maintain-

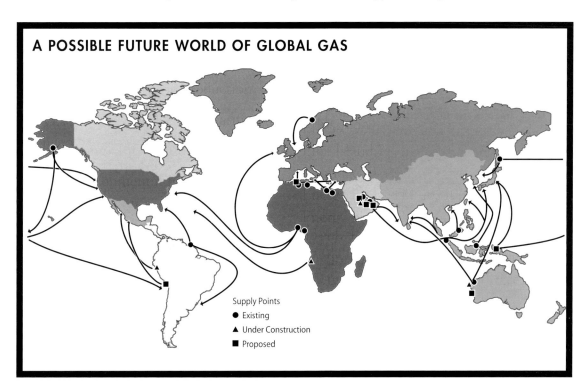

ing prices that do not constrain market growth. In fact, some observers believe that the LNG industry is poised to consistently deliver $4/MMBtu natural gas (equivalent to $25/barrel oil) to any market in the world within the next few years. Certainly if the current evolution of technology makes this possible, and political or financial shocks don't intervene, we may soon see LNG take center stage as a critical supply source for Atlantic markets much as it has done for Asian markets over the last decades. In the near term, we are likely to see a number of new liquefaction, tanker and regasification projects constructed and a growing dependence on LNG-delivered supplies in the U.K., Western Europe, the developing economies of Asia, and some countries in the Americas. And in the long term, we may well see an industry with all the rewards and pitfalls of today's global oil industry.

A

APPENDIX A: GLOSSARY

Absolute pressure — Gauge pressure plus barometric or atmospheric pressure. Absolute pressure can be zero only in a perfect vacuum.

Aquifer — A geologic formation containing water. Natural gas is often found in the presence of aquifers.

Associated gas — Natural gas found in contact with or dissolved in crude oil.

Atmospheric pressure — The pressure due to the weight of air and water vapor on the earth's surface. The average atmospheric pressure at sea level is 14.696 psi.

Auto-refrigeration — The process in which LNG is kept at its boiling point, so that any added heat is countered by energy lost from boil-off.

Balancing — The act of matching volumes of gas received by a pipeline or LDC to the volumes of gas removed from the pipeline or LDC at the delivery point.

Base load — Natural gas usage that is constant throughout a specified time period.

Basis differential — The difference in price between an index and the cash price of the same commodity. Often basis is used to refer to the difference in price between an index based at a trading hub and the cash price at another physical location.

Bcf — Billions of cubic feet, a measurement of volume of natural gas.

Boil-off — LNG that is lost during transport or storage due to natural revaporization.

British thermal unit (Btu) — The quantity of heat required to raise the temperature of one pound of water by one degree Fahrenheit.

Burnertip — The point where gas is consumed.

Butane — A component of natural gas that is typically extracted at a processing plant and sold separately.

Calorimeter — An instrument for determining the heating value of a fuel.

Capacity — The maximum amount of natural gas that can be produced, transported, stored, distributed, or utilized in a given period of time.

APPENDIX A: GLOSSARY

Cap rock — An impermeable rock layer that prevents gas from escaping out of a trap.

Carbon dioxide — A by-product of natural gas combustion and also an impurity sometimes found in natural gas.

Cargo arbitrage — The act of trading LNG ship cargos while they are under transport to reduce overall costs of transportation.

Citygate — The point at which gas is received into the LDC distribution system.

Compressed natural gas (CNG) — Natural gas in its gaseous state that has been compressed. CNG is used as a fuel for vehicles.

Condensate — A low-density, high-API gravity liquid/hydrocarbon mixture that generally occurs in association with natural gas.

Cryogenics — A branch of physics that deals with very low temperatures.

Cryogenic liquid — A liquefied gas that is kept in its liquid state at very low temperatures and has a normal boiling point below –130 degrees F (–90 degrees C).

Cubic foot — A common gas volume measurement. The amount of gas required to fill a volume of one cubic foot under stated conditions of temperature, pressure and water vapor.

Cubic meter — A common gas volume measurement. The amount of gas required to fill a volume of one cubic meter under stated conditions of temperature, pressure and water vapor.

Cushion gas — A volume of gas that must always be present in a storage field to maintain adequate pressure to cycle gas.

Cycling — Injecting and withdrawing gas from storage.

Deliverability — The amount of natural gas a well, field, pipeline, or distribution system can supply in a given period of time.

Delivery point — The location to which gas is transported.

Demand — The rate at which gas is delivered to or by a system at a specific instant or averaged over a period of time.

Deregulation — The process of decreasing or eliminating government regulatory control over industries and allowing competitive forces to drive the market.

Distribution system — A gas pipeline normally operating at pressures of 60 pounds per square inch or less that brings gas from the higher pressure transmission line to the customer.

Double-hulled ships — Tankers that are specially designed to have two layers of hull to prevent leakage or rupture in an accident.

Downstream — Commercial gas operations that are closer to the market.

Dry gas — Natural gas that doesn't contain liquid hydrocarbons.

Enhanced oil recovery (EOR) fields — Reservoirs in which secondary recovery techniques are used to extract oil.

End user — The ultimate consumer of gas.

Ethane — A component of natural gas.

Exploration — The process of finding natural gas.

Ex ship — Sale of LNG where the delivery point is the location where the LNG is off-loaded from the tanker.

Feedstock — Raw material such as natural gas used to manufacture chemicals made from petroleum.

FERC — The Federal Energy Regulatory Commission, the federal body that regulates interstate transmission of gas and electricity.

Freight on Board (F.O.B.) — Sale of LNG where the delivery point is the outlet of the liquefaction facility.

Fossil fuel — Any fuel created by the decomposition of organic matter, including natural gas, oil and coal.

Gas marketer — See Marketer.

Gas processing — The act of cleaning impurities and other substances out of natural gas streams and creating the desired heat content.

Gas-to-air ratio — The percentage of natural gas to air in a fixed volume.

Gathering system — A system of small pipelines that collects gas from individual lease facilities for delivery to a mainline system.

Gauge pressure — The pressure generally shown by measuring devices. This is the pressure in excess of that exerted by the atmosphere.

Heat content — The amount of useful energy measured in British Thermal Units (btu) per volume of gas.

Heating value — The amount of energy content contained within a specific volume

APPENDIX A: GLOSSARY

of natural gas. Commonly measured in units of Btu per Mcf.

Henry Hub — The location of a major pipeline hub in Louisiana. This location is used as the primary natural gas price index point in the U.S. and is the location where delivery occurs for NYMEX natural gas futures.

Hub — A physical location where multiple pipelines interconnect and where buyers and sellers can make transactions.

Hydrocarbon — Chemical compound containing carbon and hydrogen.

Impermeable rock — Rock that does not allow gas or fluid to migrate through it.

Index — A calculated number designed to represent the average price of gas bought and sold at a specific location.

Injection — The process by which natural gas is forced back into a reservoir for storage purposes.

Interconnection — The facilities that connect two pipelines.

Interstate pipeline — A federally regulated pipeline that is engaged in moving gas in interstate commerce.

Intrastate pipeline — A pipeline that is regulated by the state public utilities commission. Intrastate pipelines cannot transport gas that will ultimately be delivered outside the state in which the pipeline is regulated.

Line pack — The inventory of natural gas in a pipeline.

Liquefaction — The process of altering the state of natural gas from gas to liquid (done by cooling the gas below approximately –260 degrees F (–127 degrees C) at atmospheric temperature.

Liquefied natural gas (LNG) — Natural gas that is stored and transported in liquid form, at atmospheric pressure, at a temperature of approximately –260 degrees F (–127 degrees C).

Liquefied petroleum gas (LPG) — Gas consisting primarily of propane, propylene, butane, and butylene in various mixtures.

LNG tanker — A tanker ship designed to transport LNG. An LNG tanker must have insulation and cryogenic facilities to keep the LNG cool enough to stay in liquid form.

Local distribution company (LDC) — The regulated distribution company that moves natural gas from the interstate pipeline to end-use customers and often provides bundled gas supply service to residential and small commercial customers.

Mainline system — A gas pipeline, normally operating at pressures greater than 60 pounds per square inch, that transports gas from other mainline systems or gathering systems to lower pressure distribution and local transmission systems. Also known as a transmission line or backbone system.

Market center — A physical location where buyers and sellers make transactions (this may or may not also be a hub).

Marketer — An entity that buys gas, arranges for its transportation and then resells the gas to end users or other gas purchasers.

Mercaptan — A harmless odor injected into natural gas giving it the smell of rotten eggs.

Meter — A device used to measure natural gas as it moves from one point on the system to another.

Methane — The main component of natural gas.

Midstream — Commercial gas operations that are generally associated with the transmission aspect of the industry.

MMBtu — Million British thermal units, a measurement of the energy content of natural gas.

Mtpa — Million tonnes per annum, a measure of LNG volume moved or created per year. One tonne (metric ton) is approximately 2.47 cubic meters of LNG.

Monopoly — A marketplace characterized by only one seller with a unique product.

Muni — See municipal utility.

Municipal utility — A utility owned and operated by a municipality or a group of municipalities.

Natural gas — A combustible gaseous mixture of simple hydrocarbon compounds, primarily methane.

Natural gas liquids — Hydrocarbons found in raw natural gas that are liquid at ambient temperatures and pressures. Includes ethane, propane, butane, and pentanes.

Offshore terminal — An LNG terminal that is located at an offshore location rather than on land.

Off-peak — The period of a day, week, month, or year when demand is at its lowest.

APPENDIX A: GLOSSARY

Open access — Rules set by regulators that require owners of facilities to make the facilities available to any market participant under consistent terms and prices. The opposite of proprietary use.

Peak — The period of a day, week, month, or year when demand is at its highest.

Peak load — The maximum demand for gas in a given period of time (usually monthly or annually).

Peak-shaving — Augmenting the normal supply of gas during peak or emergency periods from another source (such as gas in storage) where it may have been stored during lower usage periods. Using these supplemental sources prevents pipelines from having to expand their delivery facilities just to accommodate short periods of extremely high demand.

Peak-shaving storage facility — A facility on the gas distribution system where LNG is stored and re-vaporized into gas for injection into the distribution system on days of high demand. Many peak-shaving storage facilities also include liquefaction facilities.

Pounds per square inch (psi) — A unit of pressure. At one psi, a force of one pound-force is applied to an area of one square inch.

Producer — An entity that operates wells to bring gas from reservoirs into the gathering system.

Production — The amount of natural gas that is taken out of a reserve and made available to the marketplace within a defined period of time.

Propane — A component of natural gas that is typically extracted at a processing plant and sold separately.

Proprietary use — Rules that allow the owner of a facility to use that facility for its own corporate needs and to refuse to serve other market participants in a like manner. The opposite of open access.

Public utility — A regulated entity that supplies the general public with an essential service such as electricity, natural gas, water, or telephone.

Rate base — The net investment in facilities, equipment and other property a utility has constructed or purchased to provide utility service to its customers.

Receipt point — The point on a pipeline system at which gas is taken into the system.

Regasification — The process of altering the state of natural gas from liquid to gas by warming the gas above –260 degrees F (–127 degrees C).

Regulation — The myriad of rules or orders issued by state or federal agencies that dictate how gas service is provided to customers. Note that this term is also used in gas operations to describe the act of managing gas pressures in the pipe.

Reserves — The quantity of natural gas that is economically recoverable with the use of current technology.

Reservoir — An underground deposit of natural gas.

Resources — Quantities of gas – discovered or undiscovered – that can reasonably be expected to exist.

Retail marketer — A firm that sells products and services directly to end users.

Return on investment (ROI) — Ratio of net profit after taxes to the investment used to make the net profit.

Sales and purchase agreement (SPA) — The standard agreement specifying the terms and conditions for sales of LNG.

Salt cavern storage — An underground salt cavern formation that has been hollowed out for use in storing natural gas.

Send-out — The quantity of gas delivered by a plant or system during a specified period of time.

Spot market — The short-term market for natural gas.

Storage — A means of maintaining gas in reserve for future demand, either through injection as gas into a storage field or by holding as LNG in a tank.

Storage tank — A tank designed to store LNG. LNG storage tanks are double-walled with insulation between the walls to keep the LNG cold.

Stranded gas — Gas reserves that have been proven, but are located in a region that has neither sufficient demand to use the gas nor infrastructure to deliver the gas to a region with sufficient demand.

Supply basin — A geographical area where numerous reservoirs are located.

Take-or-pay — A contractual provision that requires a shipper to pay for service whether it was utilized or not.

Terminal — The facility where an LNG tanker off-loads the LNG, generally considered to consist of the off-loading facilities, storage, and the regasification plant.

Therm — A unit of heating value. One therm is equivalent to 100,000 Btu.

APPENDIX A: GLOSSARY

Throughput — The volume of gas flowing through a pipeline.

Tolling rates — Pricing that charges a customer a fixed rate per volume for use of a facility.

Tonnes — A measure of volume of LNG, also called metric tonnes. One tonne equals 2,204.62 lbs.

Trading point — See Market center.

Train — An individual unit in a liquefaction plant. Multiple trains are often configured in parallel to increase the capacity of a liquefaction plant.

Trap — An area of the earth's crust that has developed in such a way that it traps petroleum.

Upstream — Commercial gas operations that are generally associated with the production aspect of the industry.

Well — The hole drilled into the earth's surface to produce natural gas.

Wellhead — The point where gas is pumped from the reservoir and enters the gathering system.

Wet gas — Natural gas that produces a liquid condensate when it is brought to the surface.

Wobbe Index — The gross calorific value of a volume of gas divided by the square root of the density of the gas as compared with air.

Vaporization — The process that converts LNG back into a gaseous state.

B

APPENDIX B: LNG UNITS

1 million tonnes (liquid) = 48.7 Bcf (gas)

1 tonne (LNG) (liquid) = 53.57 MMBtu (gas)**

1 cf (gas) = .0283 cubic meters (gas)

1 cf (gas) = .000045 cubic meters (liquid)

A typical tanker holds 2.8 Bcf of gas (= 126,000 cubic meters of liquid)

1 tonne (metric ton) = 2,204.62 lb = 1.1023 short tons

1 kilocalorie (kcal) = 4.187 kilojoule (kJ) = 3.968 Btu

1 Dth = 1 MMBtu = 10 therms = 1,000,000 Btu

1 million tonnes (LNG) = 48.7 Bcf* (gas) = 1.379 billion m^3 (gas)

1 million tonnes per year (mtpa) (LNG) = 48.7 Bcf/year* (gas) = 1.379 billion m^3/year (gas)

* Assumes a specific gravity of LNG at .45

** Assumes a natural gas heating value of 1,100 Btu/cf

C

APPENDIX C: ACRONYMS

Bcf — Billion cubic feet

Btu — British thermal unit

C — Celsius

Cf — Cubic foot

CFR — Code of Federal Regulation

CGA — Canadian Gas Association

CIF — Cost, insurance, freight

CNG — Compressed natural gas

CO_2 — Carbon dioxide

DOE — U.S. Department of Energy

DOT — Department of Transportation

Dth — Decatherm

E&P — Exploration and production

EBRV — Energy Bridge™ Regasification Vessel

EIA — Energy Information Administration

EIS — Environmental Impact Statement

EOR — Enhanced oil recovery

EPA — Environmental Protection Agency

F — Fahrenheit

FERC — Federal Energy Regulatory Commission

FOB — Freight on board

APPENDIX C: ACRONYMS

FSRU — Floating storage and regasification unit

GBS — Gravity based structure

GECF — Gas Exporting Countries Forum

GJ — Gigajoule

GTL — Gas-to-liquids

ISPS — International Ship and Port Facility Security

IMO — International Maritime Organization

LDC — Local distribution company

LHG — Liquefied hazardous gas

LNG — Liquefied natural gas

LPG — Liquefied petroleum gas

M³ — Cubic meter

MAOP — Maximum allowable operating pressure

MARAD — Maritime Administration

Mcf — Thousand cubic feet

MDQ — Maximum daily quantity

MMBtu — Million British thermal units

MMcf — Million cubic feet

MMDth — Million decatherms

Mtpa — Million tonnes per annum

NFPA — National Fire Protection Agency

NGLS — Natural gas liquids

NO$_x$ — Nitrogen oxide

NYMEX — New York Mercantile Exchange

O&M — Operations and maintenance

OPEC — Organization of Petroleum Exporting Countries

ORV — Open rack vaporizer

Psi — Pounds per square inch

Psig — Pounds per square inch gauge

PUC — Public Utilities Commission

ROE — Return on equity

ROI — Return on investment

ROR — Rate of return

SCV — Submerged combustion vaporizer

SPA — Sales and purchase agreement

Tcf — Trillion cubic feet

Th — Therm

TPA — Third party access

U.K. — United Kingdom

USGS — United States Geological Survey

D

APPENDIX D: WORLDWIDE LIQUEFACTION TERMINALS

Facility Name	Capacity (mtpa)	Ownership	Start Year

Atlantic Basin – Existing Facilities[1]

Algeria

Arzew GL 4Z	1.5	Sonatrach	1964
Bethioua GL 1Z	10.5	Sonatrach	1978
Bethioua GL 2Z	0.5	Sonatrach	1981
Skikda GL 1K	0.85	Sonatrach	1972
Skikda GL 2K	2.5	Sonatrach	1981
Total Algeria	15.85		

Egypt

Egyptian LNG	7.2	BG, Egyptian General Petroleum Company, Egyptian Natural Gas Holding Company, Gaz de France, Petronas	2005
SEGAS	5.0	Egyptian General Petroleum Company, Egyptian Natural Gas Holding Company, Union Fenosa Gas	2004
Total Egypt	12.2		

Equatorial Guinea

Equatorial Guinea LNG	3.7	Marathon, Mitsui, Marubeni, Sonagas	2007
Total Equatorial Guinea	3.7		

Libya

Marsa El-Brega	0.8	Libyan National Oil Company	1970
Total Libya	0.8		

Nigeria

Bonny Island T1/T2	6.6	Nigerian National Petroleum Corp, Shell, Total, Eni	1999
Bonny Island T3	3.3	Nigerian National Petroleum Corp, Shell, Total, Eni	2002
Bonny Island T4	4.0	Nigerian National Petroleum Corp, Shell, Total, Eni	2005
Bonny Island T5	4.0	Nigerian National Petroleum Corp, Shell, Total, Eni	2006
Total Nigeria	17.9		

Norway

Snohvit	4.3	Statoil, Petoro, Total, Gaz de France, Hess, RWE-DEA	2007
Total Norway	4.3		

---

[1] All information provided in this Appendix was current as of early 2010.

APPENDIX D: WORLDWIDE LIQUEFACTION TERMINALS

Facility Name	Capacity (mtpa)	Ownership	Start Year
Trinidad and Tobago			
Atlantic LNG T1	3.0	National Gas Company of Trinidad and Tobago, BP, BG, Repsol, Suez	1999
Atlantic LNG T2	3.3	Amoco, BG, Repsol	2002
Atlantic LNG T3	3.3	Amoco, BG, Repsol	2003
Atlantic LNG T4	5.2	National Gas Company of Trinidad and Tobago, BP, BG, Repsol	2006
Total Trinidad and Tobago	14.8		

Atlantic Basin – Under Construction

Facility Name	Capacity (mtpa)	Ownership	Start Year
Algeria			
Skikda GL 1K Rebuild	4.5	Sonatrach	2011
Angola			
Angola LNG	5.2	Chevron, Sonagas, Eni, BP, Total	2012
Norway			
Skangass	0.3	Lyse, Celsius Invest AS	2010
Total Atlantic	10.0		

Middle East – Existing Facilities

Facility Name	Capacity (mtpa)	Ownership	Start Year
Oman			
Oman LNG	7.1	Government of Oman, Shell, Total, Korea LNG, Mitsubishi, Mitsui, Itochu, Partex	2000
Qalhat LNG	3.3	Government of Oman, Oman LNG, Union Fenosa, Osaka Gas, Mitsubishi, Itochu	2006
Total Oman	10.4		
Qatar			
Qatar Gas 1	9.9	Qatar Petroleum, ExxonMobil, Total, Mitsui, Marubeni	1996
RasGas T1/T2	6.6	Qatar Petroleum, ExxonMobil, Korea LNG, Itochu LNG Japan	
RasGas T3	4.7	Qatar Petroleum, ExxonMobil	2004
RasGas T4	4.7	Qatar Petroleum, ExxonMobil	2005
RasGas T5	4.7	Qatar Petroleum, ExxonMobil	2006
RasGas T6	7.8	Qatar Petroleum, ExxonMobil	2009
Total Qatar	38.4		
United Arab Emirates			
ADGAS T1/T2	3.6	Abu Dhabi National Oil Co, Mitsui, BP, Total	1977
ADGAS T3	2.3	Abu Dhabi National Oil Co, Mitsui, BP, Total	1994
Total UAE	5.9		

Facility Name	Capacity (mtpa)	Ownership	Start Year
Yemen			
Yemen LNG	6.7	Total, Hunt, Yemen Gas, SK, Kogas, Hyundai, General Authority for Social Security and Pensions	2009
Total Yemen	6.7		

Middle East – Under Construction

Facility Name	Capacity (mtpa)	Ownership	Start Year
Iran			
Iran LNG	10.8	Iran LNG Company	2012
Qatar			
Qatar Gas 2	15.6	Qatar Petroleum, ExxonMobil, Total	2010
Qatar Gas 3	7.8	Qatar Petroleum, ConocoPhillips, Mitsui	2010
QatarGas 4	7.8	Qatar Petroleum, Royal Dutch Shell	2010
RasGas T7	7.8	Qatar Petroleum, ExxonMobil	2010
Total Middle East	49.8		

Pacific Basin – Existing Facilities

Facility Name	Capacity (mtpa)	Ownership	Start Year
Australia			
Darwin LNG	3.2	ConocoPhillips, Santos, Eni, Inpex, Tokyo Electric, Tokyo Gas	2006
North West Shelf T1/T2	5.0	BHP, BP, Chevron, Mitsui, Mitsubishi, Shell, Woodside	1989
North West Shelf T3	2.5	BHP, BP, Chevron, Mitsui, Mitsubishi, Shell, Woodside	1992
North West Shelf T4	4.4	BHP, BP, Chevron, Mitsui, Mitsubishi, Shell, Woodside	2005
North West Shelf T5	4.4	BHP, BP, Chevron, Mitsui, Mitsubishi, Shell, Woodside	2008
Total Australia	19.5		
Brunei			
Brunei LNG	7.2	State of Brunei, Shell, Mitsubishi	1972
Total Brunei	7.2		
Indonesia			
Arun	5.8	Pertamina	1978
Arun Phase 1 Expansion	3.9	Pertamina	1984
Arun Phase 2 Expansion	1.9	Pertamina	1986
Bontang A/B	4.5	Pertamina	1977
Bontang C/D	4.5	Pertamina	1983
Bontang E	2.3	Pertamina	1989
Bontang F	2.5	Pertamina	1994
Bontang G	2.8	Pertamina	1996
Bontang H	2.9	Pertamina	1999
Tangguh - Indonesia	7.6	BP, CNOOC, MI Berau BV, Nippon Oil Exploration, KG Companies, LNG Japan, Talisman	2009
Total Indonesia	38.7		

APPENDIX D: WORLDWIDE LIQUEFACTION TERMINALS

Facility Name	Capacity (mtpa)	Ownership	Start Year
Malaysia			
MLNG Satu	8.1	Petronas, Mitsubishi, Sarawak State	1983
MLNG Dua	7.8	Petronas, Mitsubishi, Sarawak State, Shell	1996
MLNG Tiga	6.8	Petronas, Shell, Sarawak State, Nippon Oil, Mistubishi/Japex	2003
Total Malaysia	22.7		
Russia			
Sakhalin	9.6	Gazprom, Shell, Mitsui, Mitsubishi	2009
Total Russia	9.6		
United States			
Kenai LNG	1.4	ConocoPhillips, Marathon	1969
Total United States	1.4		

Pacific Basin – Under Construction

Facility Name	Capacity (mtpa)	Ownership	Start Year
Australia			
Pluto LNG	4.4	Woodside, Kansai Electric, Tokyo Gas	2011
Peru			
Peru LNG	4.4	Hunt Oil, SK Energy, Repsol, Marubeni	2010
Total Pacific Basin	8.8		

E

APPENDIX E: WORLDWIDE REGASIFICATION TERMINALS

Facility Name	Capacity (mtpa)	Ownership	Start Year
Asia – Existing Facilities[1]			
China			
Fujian	2.6	CNOOC, Fujian Zhongmin	2009
Guangdong	6.2	CNOOC, BP	2006
Shanghai	3.0	CNOOC, Shenergy	2009
Total China	11.8		
India			
Dahej	10.0	Petronet LNG	2004/2009
Hazira	3.5	Shell, Total	2005
Total India	13.5		
Japan			
Chita Joint Terminal	7.6	Toho Gas, Chubu Electric	1977
Chita LNG	11.5	Chubu Electric, Toho Gas	1983
Chita Midorihama	5.4	Toho Gas, Chubu Electric	2001
Fukuoka	0.9	Saibu Gas	1993
Futtsu	20.1	TEPCO	1985
Hatsukaichi	0.6	Hiroshima Gas	1995
Higashi Ohgishima	25.5	Tokyo Electric	1984
Himeji II	5.0	Osaka Gas, Kansai Electric	1984
Himeji LNG Terminal	8.5	Kansai Electric, Osaka Gas	1979
Kagoshima	0.2	Nippon Gas	1996
Kawagoe	5.5	Chubu Electric	1997
Mizushima	0.6	Chugoku Electric, Nippon, Mitsubishi	2006
Nagasaki	0.1	Saibu Gas	2003
Negishi	12.1	Tokyo Gas, TEPCO	1969
Niigata	9.0	Nihonkai LNG Co., Tohoku Electric	1984
Ohgishima	6.0	Tokyo Gas	1998
Oita	4.9	Kyushu Electric, Oita Gas	1990
Sakai	2.1	Kansai Electric	2006
Senboku I	2.5	Osaka Gas	1972
Senboku II	12.9	Osaka Gas, Kansai Electric, Nippon Steel	1977
Shin-Minato	0.3	Sendai Gas	1997
Sodegaura	29.3	Tokyo Gas, TEPCO	1973
Sodeshi	0.9	Shizuoka Gas	1997
Tobata	6.8	Kyushu Electric, Nippon Steel	1977

[1] All information provided in this Appendix was current as of early 2010.

APPENDIX E: WORLDWIDE REGASIFICATION TERMINALS

Facility Name	Capacity (mtpa)	Ownership	Start Year
Yanai	2.4	Chukogu Electric	1990
Yokkaichi LNG Center	7.1	Chubu Electric	1987
Yokkaichi Works	0.7	Toho Gas, Chubu Electric	1991
Total Japan	188.5		

Kuwait

Facility Name	Capacity (mtpa)	Ownership	Start Year
Mina Al-Ahmadi GasPort	3.0	Kuwait Petroleum Company	2009
Total Kuwait	3.0		

South Korea

Facility Name	Capacity (mtpa)	Ownership	Start Year
Inchon	27.9	Korea Gas	1996
Kwangyang	1.8	Pohang Steel	2005
Pyeongtaek	25.7	Korea Gas	1986
Tongyeong	15.9	Korea Gas	2002
Total South Korea	71.3		

Taiwan

Facility Name	Capacity (mtpa)	Ownership	Start Year
Taichung	3.0	CPC Corp	2009
Yung An	17.9	CPC Corp	1990
Total Taiwan	20.9		

Asia – Under Construction

China

Facility Name	Capacity (mtpa)	Ownership	Start Year
Binhai	3.0	CNOOC	2011
Dalian	3.0	PetroChina	2011
Tianjin	2.0	CNOOC, Guandong Yudean Group	2010
Zhejiang	3.0	CNOOC, Zhejiang Group, Ningbo Development	2011

India

Facility Name	Capacity (mtpa)	Ownership	Start Year
Dabhol	5.5	Ratnagiri LNG	2010
Kochi	2.5	Petronet	2012

Japan

Facility Name	Capacity (mtpa)	Ownership	Start Year
Naoetsu	1.0	Inpex	2014
Sakaide	3.7	Shikoku Electric, Shikoku Gas, Cosmo Oil	2010

Thailand

Facility Name	Capacity (mtpa)	Ownership	Start Year
Map Ta Phut	5.0	PTT, Electricity Generating Authority	2011
Total Asia	28.7		

Facility Name	Capacity (mtpa)	Ownership	Start Year

Europe – Existing Facilities

Belgium
Zeebrugge	6.6	GDF Suez, Publigaz, Fluxys	1987
Total Belgium	6.6		

France
Fos-Cavaou	6.0	Gaz de France, Total	2009
Fos-sur-Mer	5.1	Gaz de France	1972
Montoir de Bretagne	7.5	Gaz de France	1982
Total France	18.6		

Greece
Revithoussa	2.3	DEPA	2000
Total Greece	2.3		

Italy
Panigaglia	2.5	GNL Italia	1969
Rovigo Adriatic offshore	5.8	ExxonMobil, Qatar Terminal Limited, Edison	2009
Total Italy	8.3		

Portugal
Sines	4.0	GalpEnergia	2004
Total Portugal	4.0		

Spain
Barcelona	13.7	Enagas	1968
Bilbao	5.9	BP, Iberdola, Repsol, EVE	2003
Cartagena	7.3	Engas	1989
El Ferrol	2.6	Reganosa Group, Union Fenosa, Endesa, Sonatrach	2007
Huelva	10.0	Engas	1988
Sagunto	4.8	Union Fenosa, Iberdrola, Endesa	2007
Total Spain	44.3		

Turkey
Aliaga	4.4	Egegaz	2006
Marmara Ereglisi	4.8	Botas	1992
Total Turkey	9.2		

United Kingdom
Dragon	4.4	BG, Petronas, 4Gas	2009
Isle of Grain	9.8	National Grid Transco	2005
Teesside GasPort	3.0	Excelerate Energy	2007
Total United Kingdom	17.2		

APPENDIX E: WORLDWIDE REGASIFICATION TERMINALS

Facility Name	Capacity (mtpa)	Ownership	Start Year

Europe – Under Construction

Italy
Brindisi	6.0	BG	Uncertain
Livorno offshore	3.0	Endesa, Iride, ASA, OLT Energy, Golar	2010

Netherlands
Gate	8.8	Gasunie, Vopak	2011

Spain
El Musel	5.1	Enagas	2011
Sagunto Expansion	1.0	Union Fenosa, Iberdrola, Endesa	2012

Sweden
Nynäshamn	0.2	AGA Gas	2011

United Kingdom
Isle of Grain Expansion	5.0	National Grid Transco	2010
South Hook	7.8	Qatar Petroleum, ExxonMobil, Total	2010

Total Europe   36.9

North America – Existing Facilities

Canada
St. Johns, New Brunswick	7.5	Irving Oil, Repsol	2009

Total Canada   7.5

Dominican Republic
Andres	1.8	AES	2003

Total Dominican Republic   1.8

Mexico
Altimira, Tamulipas	3.8	Shell, Total	2006
Costa Azul, Baja California	7.5	Sempra	2008

Total Mexico   11.3

United States
Cameron LNG, LA	11.4	Sempra	2009
Cove Point, MD	13.1	Dominion	1978
Elba Island, GA	11.4	El Paso	1978
Everett, MA	6.1	Suez	1971
Freeport, TX	11.4	Michael Smith, ConocoPhillips	2008

Facility Name	Capacity (mtpa)	Ownership	Start Year
Gulf Gateway, LA offshore	3.3	Excelerate Energy	2005
Lake Charles, LA	14.0	Southern Union	1982
N.E. Gateway, MA offshore	3.0	Excelerate Energy	2008
Penuelas, PR	2.7	Gas Natural, International Power, Mitsui	2000
Sabine Pass, LA	30.5	Cheniere Energy	2008
Total United States	106.9		

North America – Under Construction

Mexico
Manzanillo	3.8	Samsung, Korea Gas, Mitsui	2010

United States
Golden Pass, TX	3.8	ExxonMobil, Qatar Petroleum	2010
Neptune LNG, MA offshore	3.8	Suez LNG	2010
Gulf LNG, MS	5.0	El Paso, Sonangol, Crest Group	2011
Total North America	16.4		

South America – Existing Facilities

Argentina
Bahia Blanca offshore	5.75	Excelerate	2008
Total Argentina	5.75		

Brazil
Guanabara Bay offshore	3.5	Petrobras	2009
Pecem offshore	1.5	Petrobras	2008
Total Brazil	5.0		

Chile
Quintero	2.5	ENAP, BG	2009
Total Chile	2.5		

South America – Under Construction

Chile
Mejillones	1.5	Codelco, GDF Suez	2010
Total South America	1.5		

F

APPENDIX D: INDEX

AES 91
Africa 107-108
Algeria 35, 90, 108
American Bureau of Shipping 38
Argentina 20-21
Atlantic Basin 9, 60
Australia 8, 18-19, 20
Belarus 16
Belgium 8, 16, 17, 57, 93
BG 91
Boil-off 38
Bolivia 20-21, 108
BP 90, 91
Brazil 20-21
Brunei 8
Btu content 6, 33, 53, 54, 60
Canada 14, 15, 17-18, 101, 109
Cheniere 91
Chevron 91
Chile 20-21
China 13-22, 101, 109
Chubu Electric 90
CIF 92
CNOOC 91
CO_2 33
Coast Guard and Maritime Administration 82
Colombia 20-21
Columbia Gas 90

Compressed natural gas 45
ConocoPhillips 91
Consumers
    Commercial 14
    Electric generation 14
    Industrial 14
    Residential 13-14
Contracts 94
Cove Point 71
Cryogenic liquid 27, 58
Deepwater Port Act of 1974 80, 82
Deepwater Port Act of 2002 80
Department of Transportation 78, 82
Dominican Republic 57
Dominion Resources 91
Dual Fuel Diesel Electric 39
Earthquake 71-72
Egypt 108
El Paso 90
Elba Island 71
Enbridge 91
Energy BridgeTM 46, 106
Energy BridgeTM Regasification Vessel 43-44, 46
Energy Information Administration, the 15
Energy Policy Act of 2005 60, 77, 78, 80, 81, 83, 84-85
Environmental concerns 63-73
Environmental Impact Statement 84-85

APPENDIX F: INDEX

Environmental issues 72
Ex-ship 92
Excelerate Energy 43-44, 91
Exmar 91
ExxonMobil 52, 90, 91
Faraday, Michael 7-8
FERC 60, 81, 84-85
Financing 98-100
    Construction financing 100
    Development financing 99-100
    Term financing 100
Fractionation 54
France 8, 16, 17, 57, 90, 101
Freight on board 92-93
Gas Exporting Countries Forum 108
Gas-to-liquids 106
Gaz de France 90, 91
Germany 16, 17
Global gas 111
Golar LNG 91
Greece 17, 57
Henry Hub 93
India 13-22, 56, 57, 101, 109
Indonesia 8, 18-19, 20, 90, 107-108
International Maritime Organization 36, 78-79
International Ship and Port Facility Security Code 79
Iran 14-15, 18-19, 20, 108
Iraq 19
Italy 8, 17, 57
Izoflex 61
Japan 18-19, 20, 53, 57, 90, 109
Kazakhstan 16
Kenai LNG Export Terminal 77
Kogas 91

Korea 56, 109
Korea Gas 90
Kyoto Protocol, the 16, 107
Libya 108
Liquefaction 25-33
    Capital costs 29-30
    Example of costs 30
    Infrastructure 30-32
    Market share 31
    Processes 27
        APCI MCR 28
        Phillips Optimized Cascade 28
    Variable costs 30
LNG
    Definition 2
    Global trade 7
    History of 7-8
    How LNG is made 3-5
    Marketplace 9
    Physical properties of 64
    Timeline 7
    Trade flows 8
    Uses for 2-3
LNG consumption 10
LNG delivery chain 4, 35, 75
LNG pool 64-65, 71
LNG production 11
LNG swaps 93
LNG trade flows 8
LNG value chain 87
LNG-FPSO 46
Low speed diesel system 39
LPG 68-69
Malaysia 8, 18-19, 20, 90
Maran 91

Maritime Transportation Security Act of 2002 78
Market structure 87
Methane Pioneer, the 7
Mexico 17-18, 20, 101
Mitsubishi 91
Mitsui 91
National Environmental Policy Act 80, 82
National Fire Protection Agency 78, 80
National Grid Transco 91
Natural gas
    Definition 1-2
    Demand 1, 13-22
    Production 15
    Reserves 15
    Resources 15
    Supply 13-22
Natural Gas Act 77
Natural gas delivery system 3
Netherlands 16, 17
Nigeria 101, 108
Norway 17, 108
NOx 33
Oil Crisis of 1973 8
Oman 20
Oman, 108
Pacific Basin 9, 102
Pakistan 20
Panama Canal 45
Perlite 37-38, 51-52
Permitting 83-85
Pertamina 90
Peru 21
Petronas 90
Pool fire 65
Portugal 17, 57

Pricing 93
    Japanese crude cocktail 93
    S-curve 93, 96
Qatar 8, 14-15, 19, 20, 108
Rapid phase transition explosion 66
Regasification 49-61
    Capital costs 55-56
    Example of costs 56
    Infrastructure 56-59
        Existing facilities 57
        Floating storage and regasification unit 58-59
        Gravity-based structure 58-59
    Operating costs 56
    Technology 49-50
        Berthing and unloading 49-50
        Double containment tank 50
        Full containment tank 50
        Single containment tank 50
        Storage 50
Regulation 75-85
    European Union 81
    Liquefaction facilities 77
    Regasification 79-80
    Shipping 78-79
    United States 81
Repsol 91
Risk management 96-98
    Risks in the LNG marketplace 97
Risks 68
Russia 14, 14-15, 17, 107-108, 109
Safety 63-73
    Historical safety of 69-70
    Marine spills 70
Sales Purchase Agreement 91
    Key provisions of 92

Samsung Heavy Industries 46
Saudi Arabia 14, 18-19
Sempra Energy 91
Shell 90, 91
Ship certification 41
Shipping 35-47
    Capital costs 41-42
    Example of costs 42
    LNG fleet 43-45
    Technology 35-38
        Hull and Containment System 36-38
        Loading and unloading 40
        Membrane tank 37, 43
        Moss sphere tank 37, 43
        Propulsion 39
    Vapor capture and cargo monitoring 38
    Variable costs 42
SOLAS Convention 79
Sonatrach 90
South Korea 18-19, 20, 57, 90
Southern Trunkline 90
Spain 8, 16, 17, 57, 101
Statoil 91
Taiwan 20, 56, 57
Tepco 91
Terrorism 67
Thailand 18-19
Third-party access 75, 80
Tokyo Gas 90, 91
TotalFinaElf 91
Tractebel/Suez 91
Train 28
   Size 28
TransCanada 91
Trinidad and Tobago 20-21, 108
Triplex 37-38

Turkey 8, 16, 20, 57
U. S. Coast Guard 70-71, 78, 79
Ukraine 16
United Arab Emirates 8, 18-19, 20
United Kingdom 7, 16, 17, 35, 57, 101
United Nations 78-79
United States 14, 15, 17-18, 20, 57, 60, 109
Units 5-7
Uruguay 20-21
Uzbekistan 16
Vapor cloud 64-65
Vapor cloud fire 65, 66
Venezuela 14, 20-21, 107-108
Von Linde, Karl 7-8
Zeebrugge Hub 93